To Don
From Ken

Steelhead

STEELHEAD

Mel Marshall

WINCHESTER PRESS

Library of Congress Catalog Card No. 72-96089
ISBN 0-87691-093-2

Published by Winchester Press
460 Park Avenue, New York 10022

Book design by Paula Wiener

Printed in the United States of America

Contents

Introduction

Anybody who writes about fishing begins with two strikes on him and the pitcher getting wound up to whiz his Sunday curve across the plate. This is because both fish and fishermen have an inborn streak of cussedness as wide as a rampaging western river. Fish delight in doing things that a writer solemnly swears they never could do; the steelhead is no exception. It quite frequently performs in a fashion that amazes veteran fishermen, causing them to shake their heads and say with a sigh, "Well, I never saw a steelhead do anything like *that* before!"

In fishermen, the cussedness results from an infallible memory. Any angler reading a book about fishing is always able to dredge up from his personal experiences an incident or two involving unpredictable fish behavior. This allows him to prove conclusively that the fellow who wrote the book is an uninformed jackass, writing out of a vast fund of ignorance and misinformation.

All anglers who read books about fishing agree that the people who write them have probably never done any fishing at all, except possibly dangling a worm on a bent pin at the end of a cane pole. If fish could read, they just might agree with the fishermen. Fortunately for writers, fish can't read or talk, and by common consent, fishermen can't be believed.

Most of my colleagues who write about fishing join me in regretting that fish can't talk, because a lot of arguments could be settled quickly if they could. On the other hand, if fish were able to communicate with the fishermen, there'd be no reason to write books about angling, and some of us might have to look for another trade or join the unemployment rolls. As long as fish can't tell us why they behave so unpredictably, there'll be room for books speculating about their behavior and trying to analyze it for the benefit of the man who enjoys the challenge of fishing.

Any book about fishing can only reflect the sum of one man's observations, experiences, and conclusions, modified by what he's learned from other anglers. In all honesty, there are few real experts on fishing. Those who have the book learning and scientific training to approach the subject in methodically clinical fashion usually don't catch any more fish than nonexperts on the occasions when they approach angling as a sport. On the other hand, the fellows who bring in consistent catches, or who take fish under conditions that stump other anglers, generally can't explain exactly how and why they're so successful.

There are a lot of learned monographs and treatises written by the scientists, but these make pretty dull reading in spite of the fact that buried in their depths are nuggets of wisdom that would help the man who just fishes for pleasure. Not that all these experts agree; they often contradict one another and sometimes even contradict themselves. Until somebody figures out a way to interview a fish, there will be unexplored and virtually unexplorable byways in our knowledge of the habits, history, reactions, and even the physical characteristics of the fish we seek for sport. This lack of knowledge inevitably reflects on the methods by which we fish; we operate on the basis of trial and error, tentative conclusions still subject to being proved.

This means that a writer can only say, "Here's how it looks to me; you may or may not agree." The chances are pretty good that not everybody will agree, because any time two or more fishermen swap viewpoints, an argument's almost certain to follow. It might be just a polite disagreement over a convivially shared bottle, but it might also wind up as a razzmatazz name-calling Donnybrook. And while these dissensions, whether polite discussions or heated arguments, usually end with expressions of mutual respect, they seldom end with mutual agreement.

Personally, I'm inclined to blame the fish for starting most of these arguments. Without half trying, I can recall plenty of occasions when fish have behaved unbelievably. I've caught wary trout in crystal-clear water after making sloppy casts that by the book should have put down every fish within ten miles. I've taken bass on wet flies in water so muddy that no fish, even one with the piscatorial equivalent of 20/20 vision, could possibly see a fly more than an inch from its nose. I've had good luck fishing from metal boats in which nervous youngsters were doing a hard-toe tap dance. I've had trout take a fly dangling between my shins while wading a stream, and have seen salmon slide out from beneath my boat and grab an anchovy floating six inches from the hull while I untangled a backlash.

This unexpected and uncooperative behavior by fish makes liars out of experts. For that reason, I shy away from claiming to be an expert on any kind of fish or fishing. What I've tried to do in this book is to pass along my own observations and those of other fishermen who have spent a lot of time and caught a reasonable quantity of fish on the brawling steelhead rivers of the U. S. western coast and on the relatively tamer streams of the Great Lakes watershed. And I've included the trained scientific observations and conclusions of quite a few fishery biologists who have studied the steelhead with the aim of increasing its numbers, and along the way have come up with information that's helpful to the steelhead fisherman.

A lot of anglers are inclined to shortchange fishery biologists as being ivory-tower types who carry on meaningless studies in splendid isolation. Nothing could be further from the truth. Most of those whose brains I've picked for steelhead, trout, or bass lore are sports anglers in their spare time; they understand that the proof of theory comes only by the test of rod and reel. And without exception, all of them are keenly conscious that the end result of their studies and tests must be to put more fish and bigger fish and better fish into the streams where other fishermen can catch them.

A lot of current developments, topped by today's growing interest in ecology, have made the fishery biologist (who's been preaching the need for ecological awareness for years) an important man to steelhead anglers. In evergrowing numbers, fishermen are seeking steelhead, as the Atlantic salmon fishery declines due to stream pollution and international outlaws taking excessive numbers of salmon in nets offshore. Today, the angler who wants the challenge of big fish in big waters looks to the Pacific Coast and Great Lakes rather than to eastern waters unless he's so solvent that he can shrug off the high cost of eastern salmon fishing.

Population growth alone has created a new generation of steelhead enthusiasts who communicate their enthusiasm to friends all over the nation. Improved transportation, the age of the jet and the double vacation, plus the lure of open waters available to everybody, are drawing more and more anglers to steelhead country. With the resurgence of Pacific Coast steelhead fishing starting in the late 1940s and the amazing development of what is virtually a new steelhead fishery in the Great Lakes states beginning in 1967, the premier game fish of fresh water is drawing new attention. Fishermen to whom the steelhead was once only a legend are now seeking the waters where they can learn for themselves the facts of steelheading. They come not only from the eastern and midwestern United States, but from European countries where there is no public fishing available on most lakes or streams.

Often the results of quick transportation are displayed with dramatic impact. A few years ago, on California's Klamath River, I found myself exchanging angling experiences with a man whose fishing trip had started less than twelve hours earlier from his home. Not too remarkable, except that his home happened to be in Copenhagen, Denmark. After a nine-hour jet flight to San Francisco, he'd chartered a small private plane to put him down on an airstrip at Orleans, a 90-minute journey; he had only to joint up his rod and walk a few hundred yards to the river.

When I remarked that Scandinavian fishing was famous, and wondered aloud why he'd spent so much in plane fares to try that in California, he grinned sadly. "At home, I would have to spend $150 to $200 a day to fish in our fjords for salmon," he explained. "In Scandinavia, fishing rights are leased out, usually to resorts or hotels or tourist agents. I can enjoy more fishing more cheaply here, where even the common people have the right to try their luck."

While this may be an uncommon example, the number of anglers meeting the steelhead for the first time increases exponentially each year. License sales to out-of-state fishermen in all the steelhead states, Great Lakes and Pacific Coast alike, attest to this increase. That the newcomers to steelheading often have indifferent luck is both lamentable and true. It's to help the newcomer as well as the veteran that this book has been written.

This isn't a book of fishing stories, except where recalling an incident that took place on a steelhead stream will emphasize a point you should remember; you'll find few anecdotes designed to impress on your mind that the author is a fine and fearless fisherman. Diffidence and modesty have nothing to do with this; I like to brag just as much as you do. The trouble is that I've told most of my stories so often that they're no longer interesting, even to me. Besides, some of my untold experiences with steelhead are so improbable that nobody but another veteran steelheader would believe them, and he'd always have a better yarn ready with which to top mine. The steelhead, you see, leaves you with unique memories.

Of course, I've got a secret hankering to write a book of fishing tales, and may, someday. But having lived in steelhead country for a number of years and having fished most of its better rivers, I've watched a lot of other fishermen streamside. Time after time, I've been impressed with the plight of the very, very good trout or bass fishermen trying to learn the quite different techniques and approaches required to take steelhead. So, this is a how-to book, and a how-not-to book as well, since the negative can be as important as the positive in fishing. It's also a why, when, and where book, and as noted earlier, occasionally veers off into some of the discoveries made by research scientists that turn out to be of value to the angler.

It wasn't until the middle 1940s that the steelhead attracted much attention by these scientific-minded gentlemen. Until then, the steelhead was pretty much North America's forgotten game fish. Very little had been written about steelheading; Zane Grey discovered the steelhead in the Rogue and Klamath rivers in the very early 1920s, and his *Tales of Freshwater Fishing* in 1928 was the first book to be devoted primarily to the subject. Grey was so fascinated by steelhead that he built himself a cabin on the Rogue to enable him to enjoy the sport more easily.

Between 1928 and today, except for a 1938 book by Claude Kreider and a short string of magazine articles, or paragraphs in general fishing books, relatively little has been written about steelhead. There were word-of-mouth stories about the glory days, such as the occasion in 1927 when Albert Brizard played 227 fish on one Klamath River riffle on a single day, but there was no real knowledge about the fish. Even as late as the 1950s the steelhead was such a stranger to anglers that the fishing editor of a national outdoor magazine insisted that the fish's name be pluralized as "steelheads," an error as gratuitous as would be "trouts" or "basses."

There was no national interest in steelhead fishing prior to the middle 1940s; that was a time when the fish had come perilously close to extinction. Almost a decade earlier, steelhead had virtually disappeared from the Great Lakes watershed through neglect as fishery biologists fought to save sport fishing from the ravages of the invading sea lamprey and alewife. In that same period, when steelhead fishing was confined to the three Pacific Coast states, the once-great runs of the western rivers were declining as urbanization and industrialization took their toll of Pacific rivers. When it appeared that the western steelhead was about to vanish completely, cries for assistance sounded from San Francisco north to British Columbia. The cries not only brought publicity and financial help to the steelhead fishery, but attracted the scientific manpower that was desperately needed.

Such men as Clarence Pautzke, Lauren Donaldson, Robert Meigs, Ernie Salo, Thor Gudjohnson, and a few others led the way in learning more about the steelhead's life and habits, which then were almost total mysteries. This was the first step; knowledge led the way to the development of methods by which the declining annual runs could be increased. More importantly, this knowledge fathered in their pioneering research was translated into action by the states of Washington, Oregon, and California. Ultimately, official state and unofficial angler pressure brought Federal funds into the effort to revive the waning steelhead fishery.

By a happy coincidence of timing, the battle with the sea lamprey was being won in the Great Lakes during the years when the Pacific Coast steelhead fishery was being revived. As a result of western pioneering, there was available to fishery management men in Michigan, Wisconsin, and Minnesota a wealth of data useful to them when in the middle 1960s they began to restore the steelhead to a place of importance in streams tributary to the Great Lakes. As a result of all this, the steelhead angler of today and of the future, whether seeking sport in the waters of the West Coast or Upper Midwest, has about a ten-to-one better chance of connecting with good fish in both winter and summer than did his predecessor of the 1940s.

There are still a lot of mysteries connected with the steelhead; you'll find these unanswered questions and some consensus guesses as to their answers when you read further on. To the fisherman, the mysteries surrounding the fish are less important than the facts we know, the primary fact being that the steelhead enters fresh water filled with a vigor unmatched by any fish except its close cousin, the Atlantic salmon. These are the only two freshwater fish that an experienced angler cannot handle with the 30 yards of flyline commonly spooled on a reel. It's not uncommon for a fresh steelhead weighing only ten or fifteen pounds to strip off 80 to 90 yards of line in its initial run after being hooked. Nor is it uncommon for a winter steelhead to make a dozen tail-dancing leaps between hooking and beaching, or for such a fish to snap a ten-pound leader with its first fierce strike.

These are the qualities that establish the steelhead as the finest freshwater fighting fish.

Fisherman, as I've pointed out, being prone to argument, may challenge this flat statement as one angler's debatable opinion. They will offer the accolade of "finest fighting fish" to the swift-water smallmouth bass or the rainbow trout or lunging muskellunge, and each will be prepared to defend his own choice to the bitter end. This is the individual angler's right and privilege, and it would be a dull and uninteresting world if there were a single unanimous opinion about everything on it. However, my award of the championship title to the steelhead isn't on the basis of theory or hearsay, as is the case with many fishing titles.

More years than I like to think about have passed since I caught my first game fish, a smallmouth bass. I was a small boy at the time, and an honest tallying of the years since then would show a total of more than a half century. During those years, I've enjoyed many kinds of fishing in many waters. Still without claiming any expert status, I've taken all the members of the trout family; brook, brown, rainbow, spotted native, cutthroat, lake, and golden. In northern, southern, eastern, and western streams and lakes I've fished for and caught largemouth, smallmouth, white, and striped bass; muskies, pike, and pickerel. My experience with the salmonoid species has included taking salmon in coastal rivers as well as in salt water, and I've tangled with the leaping tarpon and the tough-jawed alligator gar. Along the way, I've met up with almost all the panfish, catfish, carp, and a lot of roughfish that I'd just as soon forget, including suckers and squawfish.

This sampling of the fish and fishing of North America looks a lot more impressive, grouped as above into a single paragraph, than it really has been. I still don't claim to be an expert, even though in doing my fishing I've handled almost every type of tackle, from big two-handed salmon fly rods down to stubby bait-casting rods that have about as much flexibility in their action as a billiard cue. Out of curiosity, sometimes out of necessity, I've wielded antique rods of greenheart, experimental four- and five-strip bamboos, as well as rods of glass, copper, steel, aluminum, beryllium, and other unlikely substances. Long before light tackle became commonplace, I was fishing for black bass with a delicate free-spool tournament reel holding two-thread silk, mounted on the very lightest of six-foot bamboo casting rods, using my own hand-whittled plugs weighing less than a quarter ounce.

Nor does this qualify me as an expert, because all my fishing until very recently was done for fun and relaxation, not in pursuit of knowledge or for profit. And I don't catch fish every time out, as a real expert must do to maintain his unblemished standing. I have the inevitable percentage of fishless days that all anglers encounter, regardless of the efforts they put forth. All this I cite, not to seek status, but to make the point that I've caught more than one kind of fish, and all of it by way of preliminary to justify awarding the championship title to the steelhead. It's a pretty big award, and is accompanied by a sweeping statement that requires qualification.

Now, here is my ultimate justification for giving the title to the steelhead: When the question of fighting ability comes up in the endless after-fishing discussions anglers have, the only fishermen who deny that the steelhead deserves the champsionship title are those who have never caught one.

Think about it for a minute. The man who holds out for the smallmouth bass as being the "fightingest" fish is generally drawing his comparison between bass and trout. The angler who cries the praises of the rainbow has quite probably limited his experiences to trout, perhaps to trout and bass with small side excursions after muskie and pike. But the man who has fished widely, who has caught a good, representative assortment of freshwater game fish, will not argue the point. He concedes that the winter-run steelhead is the most challenging fish an angler can encounter in the fresh waters of North America.

There's really only one way to prove or disprove the merits of the award to your own satisfaction, and that is to meet the steelhead yourself. Make its acquaintance on a cold winter's day when the wind is swooping along the banks of a big river flowing fast and green between shelving shores of ice-crusted gravel. Hook your fish, and if you successfully meet the challenge of taming its repeated leaps and long line-stripping runs, there's little doubt but what you'll find that you've been hooked, too. Time after time you will be drawn back to the banks of those harsh green rivers, to pit your wits, your strength, and your skill against the gamest fish of all—the steelhead.

Welcome to the club.

1

Meet the Steelhead

It was probably an Indian named Ab or Uhg or Ish who caught the first steelhead taken by man. All Indian tribal lore has fishing legends that go back to the misty reaches of prerecorded time; where their home territories contained fishable waters, all Indians became skilled fishermen. To feed themselves during the winter months, the coastal tribes of the Pacific Northwest depended more than did most others on harvesting the fish that came up the rivers in autumn. Salmon and steelhead both enter the western rivers for their spawning journeys at about the same time; the runs begin with a trickle of fish swimming upstream late in the summer and peak during the midwinter months.

Survival, man's strongest instinct, taught the Indian where and how and when to fish, taught him that it was necessary to think like a fish if he wanted to be sure of a good catch. This is something learned only sketchily by the average sports fisherman; he looks on fishing as a hobby, a thrill, an art, a relaxation, an escape from normal routines. But to be a successful fisherman, it's necessary to understand something about the fish you want to catch. The Indians understood this and studied the habits of fish much as we do today, their primitive research activities motivated by the instinct to survive.

Ab and Ish had no laboratories, kept no charts and compiled no statistics. They lacked the facilities for communicating and comparing their discoveries with others engaged in the same pursuit, so their learning was accumulated much more slowly than that of today's fishery biologist. Their methods, though, were much the same. Research into the habits of fish is as empirical today as it was in the days of Ab and Ish, its conclusions based on deductions drawn from observation. All that has changed is the ease with which conclusions can be compared between different researchers.

For a clear understanding of the knowledge we have today of the steelhead's habits and history, we must begin with a detour into those of the salmon. The Pacific salmon is unique among anadromous fishes, those which divide their lives between fresh and salt water, in that it dies almost immediately after spawning. Until relatively few years ago, almost every river flowing into the Pacific supported salmon and steelhead runs, the fish moving upstream to gravel-bedded shallows where they laid their eggs. At the end of the spawning season, the riffle bottoms of creeks tributary to the rivers were once literally paved with the carcasses of spawned-out salmon. It is this characteristic of the salmon dying after spawning that ichthyologists and anthropologists conclude was responsible for the creation of the Pacific coast's aboriginal salmon fishery.

Along the headwaters of some clear creek, their deductions run, a remote ancestor of Ab or Ish must have scooped up a spent salmon where it lay gasping out its last moments of life. Though the fish's flesh was flabby and soft, it was food, and to the prehistoric aborigine all food was precious. As the decades grew to centuries, the Indians learned that the further downstream the salmon were picked up, the better their flesh; they learned, too, that the firm flesh of fish taken before spawning could be preserved for the winter if it was rubbed with salt from the rims of tidal pools and dried in the sun. So, ultimately, the Indians learned to make nets of vines and fibers, to weave small branches into weirs that trapped the fresh-run fish on their upstream journey.

Eventually this led to the establishment of fishing stations, some the exclusive property of one tribe, others shared by several tribes. In the months when the fish were moving, all intertribal wars, arguments and differences were ignored and pushed aside, since survival of all the tribes depended on all of them working side by side to harvest the fish before the runs ended. Parenthetically, all the treaties made between whites and Indians in the Pacific coastal area recognized the rights of the Indians to these fishing stations, and a new period of ill feeling between the two races erupted during the 1960s when the whites tried to abrogate these long-held fishing rights.

Some cynical fishermen today suggest that we would be richer in many ways if our ancestors had taken the fishing rights and left the land to the Indians. The suggestion may be true as well as being the bitter comment of those disgusted by watching misuse of the land diminish the once-great runs of fish that entered the rivers. As early as the 1920s, water pollution and the drying-up of streams by diverting their flow to agricultural irrigation had ended steelhead and salmon runs in Pacific Coast streams south of San Francisco Bay, though old records indicate that both species had once spawned in rivers as far south as San Diego.

Both on the Pacific Coast and the Great Lakes area, logging operations that silted and blocked spawning beds and dams that denied fish access to the spawning areas combined to send once-large steelhead runs into a decline that became almost total before it could be reversed. And in both regions the sewage and garbage of cities combined with industrial wastes in thoughtless pollution of formerly clean waters. Only when anglers and other conservation-minded individuals began buttonholing politicians were stream preservation requirements imposed and fish ladders built on dams. Belatedly, the civilized white man began to treat his rivers with the respect that had been given the streams by the descendants of Ab and Ish, who looked on water as a source of life and food for all, to be treasured and preserved.

Now, our detours concluded, we are back to the Indians who caught the first steelhead. Food being their primary objective, the Indians did not consider the steelhead an important fish, or even a separate species; even today, their language has no equivalent for "steelhead"; the fish is called "little salmon" by them. Ab, Ish, and their kin wanted big fish in their nets and weirs. Steelhead will weigh consistently in the six- to twelve-pound range. Even a big one seldom tops 20 pounds, and the largest on record is a 46-pound monster taken in 1923 from Oregon's Deschutes River. Salmon, on the other hand, are medium-sized at fifteen pounds, and will average between 25 and 30. The first steelhead, taken by Ab and Ish and their fellows, were not greatly prized by them; the Indians were after food, not sport.

Sport fishing, in fact, came late to the Pacific Northwest; the first settlers had the same survival problems that the Indians faced, and shared the tribesmen's attitude toward fish. Dried salmon meant food for winter, and the bigger the fish, the better. Even as time went on, sport fishing was not very highly regarded. In the frame of reference of the early days, sport in the Pacific West meant shooting dangerous game such as bear or mountain lions. Ducks, pigeons, elk, deer, and fish were too plentiful to be a challenge to the sportsmen of the day; until the late 1800s these species were not considered game to be hunted, but food to be harvested. Generally, boys too young to be allowed to take part in the hunting that adults called sport were sent to handle the fish harvest, with pitchforks in the upper, shallow reaches of rivers and creeks.

There must have been a few freaks among the early settlers, men who brought with them the tradition of fishing with rod and reel, but they kept remarkably quiet about it. We will never know the identity of the first man to feel the leaping plunge of a steelhead transmitted through an arcing rod, or the first to cast a metal lure, or to discover that the fish would take a fly. He was without doubt an angler transplanted from the East, nostalgically trying to raise a trout in unfamiliar waters, and the fish he took was probably a summer steelhead rather than one of the bigger, more active winter-run fish.

In the states bordering the Great Lakes a sports fishing tradition was in existence prior to the first steelhead planting. However, anglers wetting their lines for the first time in Pacific Coast steelhead rivers and trout fishermen working the streams flowing into the Great Lakes made little or no distinction between steelhead and trout in the early days. When an early-day fisherman hooked a steelhead he simply thought he'd taken a rainbow trout of tremendous size and fighting ability, for until the late 1930s the belief still persisted that a steelhead is nothing more or less than a rainbow trout that has journeyed into ocean or lake waters.

There is still some discussion on this point, though it is no longer a matter of hot debate. Fish biologists and ichthyologists are not quite through debating the exact taxonomy of the steelhead, but the majority opinion is pretty well settled. There is general agreement that the steelhead is a true subspecies of the family Salmonidae, akin to the rainbow trout, but more closely kin to the Atlantic salmon.

Certain aspects of the distinguishing characteristics of the steelhead are still in process of being unraveled. Physically, there is little difference between a mature steelhead and a mature rainbow trout, and biologists have been able to find no difference whatever between the young of the two species. Mature steelhead returning to streams to spawn will generally have sides and bellies of pure silver and gray or gray-green backs bearing the characteristic small dark dots of the salmonoids. As steelhead move upstream, their coloration becomes that typical of the rainbow trout, stripes of purple-tinged crimson along the sides. The color deepens in intensity as their time to spawn comes closer, and fish that will spawn near headwaters may come already colored into the rivers, while the coloring is acquired much later by steelhead that must make a long trip to a spawning bed in a distant creek.

Body contours of steelhead and rainbow trout are identical to the eye; both have the salmonoid configuration of small head, deep body, squared tail, and tiny, almost invisible scales. There are important unseen internal differences, though, as well as differences in habit; these will be noted later. The chief distinction between steelhead and rainbow is the steelhead's urge to migrate into big water—the Pacific Ocean or Great Lakes depending on where its eggs hatched—but this is only one of several differences between them.

Before going further, it might be helpful to place the steelhead properly in the noble family to which it belongs. The taxonomy of natural science follows the Chinese fashion of putting the last or family name first, with other names following. And when discussing a subspecies in familiar terms, only its secondary names are used, much as humans use nicknames among themselves. In placing the steelhead in its family, then, we begin with the Salmonoidea, that big suborder embracing all salmonoid fishes. Within this suborder, the steelhead and its closest relatives belong to the genus *Salmo* of the family Salmonidae.

In the *Salmo* grouping are the Atlantic salmon, the European sea-trout, and the rainbow trout; agreement is complete that it is in this genus that the steelhead belongs. When the subspecies begin to be classified, opinions begin to differ. The rainbow's formal name is *Salmo irideus*, and it has no other, but different authorities identify the steelhead as *Salmo irideus gairdneri*, *Salmo gairdneri*, and *Salmo gairdneri gairdneri*. Since this isn't a scientific treatise and since the authorities aren't in full agreement anyhow, we can split the difference and from this point on refer to the steelhead as *Salmo irideus gairdneri*, when it becomes necessary to use a formal name.

To make the relationship between the Salmonidae as clear as possible, let's look at the family fairly closely. To the genus *Salmo* belong the Atlantic salmon, *S. salar*; the European sea-trout, *S. trutta*; the brown trout, *S. fario*; the cutthroat, *S. clarkii*; the fabled golden trout of the High Sierra, *S. rooseveltii*; and as we've seen, the rainbow and steelhead, *S. irideus* and *S. irideus gairdneri*. There are other members of the *Salmo* clan, but these are the best known; there are also many other Salmonidae which are frequently confused with the *Salmo*. Chief among these are the brook trout, which is a *Salvelineus*; the lake trout, which is a *Ceratodus;* and the Pacific salmon, which is *Oncorhynchus*, and which includes as subspecies the coho, sockeye, and king salmon. The only true freshwater trout are the brown, the rainbow, the golden, and the lake trout; these cannot adapt to salt water. All the other Salmonidae are anadromous, they have the ability to survive in the ocean's salty waters, even though not all of them go to sea.

Ichthyologists deduce that all of the Salmonidae descend from a common ancestor, some fish that in creation's dawning days made its home in salt water during its entire life-span. Eventually, this fish learned that its offspring had a better chance to survive if they emerged from their eggs in the shallow, brackish waters of the ocean's estuaries rather than in the open sea. The Salmonidae began going up into the bays to spawn. As century followed century the trickling of waters from rains, melting snow and glaciers, sent fresh water racing downhill, cutting streambeds into the bays, and the ancestor fish began moving progressively further upstream. Eventually, their spawning came to take place in the very headwaters of the streams, in gravel-bedded creeks or the sheltered margins of lakes.

Then there came a day when the earth heaved and new ground contours formed, and some of the streams up which the ancestor Salmonidae has been accustomed to travel, some of the lakes in which they spawned, were cut off from access to the ocean. Through what must have been an agonizing period of acclimatization, a percentage of the ancestors and their fry survived and became what are today the trout of fresh water. Others, free in the ocean during the upheavals, retained their spawning habits unchanged and became what are today's anadromous fish.

There was more than one such period of earth change, of course, for there is no fixed line that can be drawn to separate the ocean-visiting Salmonidae from those which must stay in fresh water all their lives. A number of years ago, rainbow trout from a completely landlocked lake in Montana were used by the state of Washington to restock its coastal rivers, and many of these trout went to sea and returned as steelhead. Other rainbows from the same source stayed on in the rivers.

To the layman, this appears confusing, but to the biologists it provided clear proof of their theory that however closely related they might be, the rainbow trout and the steelhead are different species. Landlocked or not, they say, the Montana lakes held both species of fish, and when given access to the ocean the steelhead strain migrated while the rainbows stayed behind. Steelhead and rainbow will probably continue to be confused in the minds of fishermen, however, the confusion compounded by the fact that there are cutthroat trout in Pacific streams which migrate to the sea, and some of the *Salvelineus* subspecies also venture into the ocean.

Common physiological characteristics of the Salmonidae are shared by all the subspecies. For instance, all of them must have a salt content of .075 percent in their body fluids. This balance is maintained by the gills and kidneys and is controlled by the fish's thyroid gland. In lakes and streams, the kidneys act as a miniature salt distillery and from water brought in through the gills extract the quantity of salt necessary to maintain the required .075 percent in the body fluids of the fish. Freshwater Salmonidae cannot alter, reverse, or change this metabolic process; if put into the ocean, with its three to four percent salt content, the freshwater trout dies, literally salted to death.

But anadromous members of the Salmonidae are able to reverse the kidney functions. When in salt water, their kidneys extract the excess salt and excrete it as waste, and the .075 percent salt content of the fish's body fluids remains unchanged. Some of the anadromous Salmonidae can change their kidney functions repeatedly, making the transition from salt water to fresh and back again to salt water an indefinite number of times. Among these are the steelhead and the Atlantic salmon.

Ability to reverse the metabolic process more than once in a lifetime seems limited to a few selected members of the genus *Salmo* and denied to others; the ability is also denied to the *Oncorhynchus* salmonoids. Coho and chinook salmon, which are of the genus *Oncorhynchus*, can make the transformation only once during their life-cycle, the one time being when they migrate as immature fish into the ocean. Nor do fish belonging to the *Oncorhynchus* branch of the Salmonidae have the ability of the Atlantic salmon and steelhead to survive after spawning. The life-cycle of all the *Oncorhynchus* salmonoids is linked in some as-yet-unexplained fashion with the reproductive function of these fish. Once eggs are generated in the body of the female and milt in the body of the male, the fish die even though the ripened eggs and milt may not have been fruitfully discharged.

Steelhead do not die in fresh water, but in the ocean. At least that is the deduction; nobody really knows the facts. A few spawned-out steelhead do die in streams, but these are fish that have starved themselves while in fresh water and have lost more than 50 percent of their original body weight. The majority of steelhead will, if they get past the fishermen on the banks, return to the ocean after spawning and make a half dozen round trips between salt water and fresh before vanishing at last in the ocean.

Tagging studies have established that a steelhead's life-span is five to seven years. Returning steelhead, grown to maturity in the sea, will spawn a maximum of four times; they may return to fresh water for another year or two, but do not spawn on their final upstream runs. And no tagged fish has been observed past the seven-year span.

All steelhead do not return on an exact annual cycle. Two or more years may go by between their returns to fresh water. After spawning, the mature fish will stay in the river or creek for perhaps a few weeks, perhaps a few months, sometimes for as long as a year. If the fish has retained at least half its original weight after spawning, its survival for another year seems guaranteed, unless while at sea it falls victim to one of the many predators that prey on ocean fish.

That steelhead die at sea is accepted generally as a fact; whether old age kills them peacefully, or whether aging reduces their ability to evade bigger fish pursuing them as food has not been established. There is a possibility that the steelhead's salting-desalting cycle cannot be reversed indefinitely. This fish may, on its last trip into the ocean, be unable to change its kidneys to reject salt, the opposite fate of the Pacific salmon.

Exactly what spells the end of the steelhead's life, whether it is the normal degeneration of age or its inability to cope with the sea's essentially feral life, is just one of the mysteries still surrounding the fish. Nobody knows where the steelhead go when they enter the ocean; what routes they travel to what destinations and what senses lead them back to the stream where they were spawned are subjects for speculation. We simply do not know whether steelhead stay within the relative shallows of the 100-mile-wide continental shelf, whether they plunge into the Pacific's great depths just beyond that shelf, or whether they journey thousands of miles north or south or west during their ocean stays.

Nor do we know how the steelhead manage to escape the hooks and nets of the saltwater fishermen. Commercial fishing activity in the Pacific is a continuous affair. There are handline fishermen, drift-net fishermen, and trawlers dragging their all-gathering purse seines at work all through each year. There are also surf fishermen and dory fishermen seeking sport in its waters most of the year, casting and trolling near the mouths of the streams up which the steelhead will swim, especially during the periods when both steelhead and salmon are gathering offshore for their spawning runs. Yet, only three catches of steelhead by either sports or commercial fishermen in ocean waters have ever been recorded.

In the Great Lakes, steelhead are not as elusive as they are in the ocean. Lakes Michigan, Superior, and Huron provide a very productive offshore fishery that extends for several miles along the shoreline on both sides of rivermouths and includes the bays or lakes in which the streams terminate. In some areas, steelhead are taken as far as three to five miles offshore as well. Why steelhead should be catchable in these areas of the Great Lakes and shun baits and lures in similar Pacific Ocean areas is one of the still unresolved mysteries surrounding the fish. The decisive factors may be water depth, salinity, temperature, or the action of bottom currents or a combination of several of these influences; the factors may equally well be influences as yet unknown and unconsidered. The question is yet to be answered.

To complete the roster of mysteries, the failure of steelhead to survive in the Atlantic must be noted. Inspired by the success achieved in transplanting striped bass, a fish native to the Atlantic, into the Pacific, repeated efforts have been made to duplicate the procedure and establish steelhead runs in east coast rivers. The latest such extensive attempt was made by the state of New Jersey over a six-year span beginning in the late 1950s. The techniques used were those which had been successfully developed in restocking western streams: a mixture of yearlings, fingerlings, and mature fish was released at annual intervals in the headwaters of selected rivers and fertilized eggs were hatched upstream, the fry being allowed to swim down to the ocean. The theory—which worked in the west—was that a percentage of the fish would return to the rivers to spawn. The efforts failed, and no one knows why. Differences in salt content and average water temperatures between the Atlantic and Pacific oceans have been advanced as theories for the failure, but the theories remain unproved.

Fishery biologists have arrived at what seems to be a proved explanation of the irregular spawning cycle of the steelhead, which keeps some fish in the ocean for two or three years before their first spawning trip. This, the biologists deduce, is nature's way of ensuring that the species will survive such catastrophes as a temporary closing of all rivermouths or the destruction of all spawning beds by some cataclysmic earth upheaval. Spacing or staggering the spawning cycle means that there will always be steelhead trying to enter the rivers, a bit of nature's foresight for which all anglers should be grateful.

As an extension of this staggered spawning cycle, young steelhead follow an irregular schedule in entering the ocean from the streams where they hatched. This is not typical of other anadromous fish, which head in schools for the sea at a predictable point in their growth. Some baby steelhead stay in the rivers as long as two years after leaving the egg, others make a token trip as far as brackish water where rivers and ocean meet, and return to the spawning beds with the mature fish. The young steelhead are incapable of spawning, though. They hang around the nests until the mature fish begin to move downstream, and follow them into salt water.

One strain of steelhead is the exception to the staggered return rule. During his experiments with restocking and propagation in Washington state in the early 1950s, Clarence Pautzke discovered that steelhead from the natural spawning in Chambers Creek moved on a highly predictable calendar. Invariably, Chambers Creek steel-head sought the ocean the year after they hatched, and always during the months of March, April, and May.

Pautzke's discovery of the Chambers Creek steelhead strain was an important point in the success he was to have in reviving Washington's declining steelhead runs. He had already determined that a major cause of the dwindling numbers of steelhead was the number of young sea-bound fish being taken each year by anglers, who were mistaking them for trout. The anglers were blameless, to be sure, since even the biologist's trained eye could not distinguish between the two. But, once he had satisfied himself as to the absolute pre-dictability of the Chambers Creek steelhead's movements, Pautzke closed the state's rivers to all fishing during the three months when the young steelhead were moving downstream. The result was a dramatic increase in Washington's steelhead runs during the years that followed.

Other Western states began to use—and are still using—Chambers Creek steelhead, and following a policy of closing selected steelhead rivers to trout fishing during March, April, and May. At the same time, all the steelhead states began paying more attention to these fish. Experiments were begun with propagation in natural as well as man-made pools and lagoons. Hatchery facilities that had been de-voted exclusively to propagating trout and salmon by the egg-and-milt-stripping process were switched, at least partly, to steelhead propagation. While methods varied from one state to another, the objective was always the same: to increase the size of the steelhead runs. Almost everywhere, the results beginning in the late 1950s were dramatic.

To give just one set of statistics, the steelhead count made each year at Winchester Dam on Oregon's North Umpqua River tallied a disappointing annual average of only 2400 fish between 1956 and 1960. The annual average count for 1966 to 1970 was 9300 fish. Hatchery smolts, identifiable by tags or pattern-clipped fins, ac-counted for 6600 mature steelhead in the 1966 to 1970 figures, or 71 percent of the total run. Figures from other rivers in all of the Pacific Coast states are comparable to those of the Umpqua.

Increases of this magnitude would probably not be possible if the steelhead was like other game fish. Trout, bass, pike, muskie, grow to maturity in a single small area of a stream or lake, and when their water is overstocked the fish population exceeds the amount of food needed to sustain them in healthy growth. The steelhead, though, is not a resident, but a commuter. During the period of its greatest growth, from yearling or smolt to maturity, the steelhead that goes into the Pacific gets its growth from the shrimp and forage fish so plentiful in that ocean and the steelhead that migrates into the deep, cold waters of the Great Lakes grows big on the alewives that abound there. In both areas, the steelhead spends little time in the rivers, and during its brief period of residence places no strain on the food resources available in the streams.

Actually, there seems to be no practical limit to the number of mature steelhead that a river can support on the fish's upstream spawning runs. Contrary to early belief, steelhead do eat while moving upstream, but the spawners are more interested in reaching their destination than in stopping for a snack along the way. Even later, during the time they spend in fresh water after having spawned, food is of little interest to them.

Stomach examinations of both male and female steelhead taken while moving upstream to spawn show that on an average day the fish eat only six or seven small morsels: a grub, a drowned insect, a stray salmon egg, a water beetle. This is roughly the equivalent of a husky six-foot man performing hard physical labor on a daily diet of two or three soda crackers.

Close observation over a three-year period of tagged steelhead that remained in fresh water after spawning has shown that these fish are equally uninterested in eating. One team of researchers observed a male steelhead that went for 34 weeks without food. This particular fish hung in a clear, shallow pool for the entire eight-month period, and started back to sea at the end of that time, having retained 50 percent of original body weight which is apparently the key to post-spawning survival of steelhead of both sexes.

Perhaps this habit of the steelhead came about because the rivers of the Pacific Northwest, while big, are not especially rich in food;

perhaps its eating pattern is only one result of the fish's spawning urge. Whatever the roots of the steelhead's diet habits, the fisherman can be grateful for them. The richness of the foods it obtains in the ocean, the active life it must lead while in the salty depths, result in the steelhead being sweet of flesh and packed with muscular power, making it a delicious fish to eat and a challenging fish to catch.

It is a heartening thing to fly over the Pacific near the mouth of a big steelhead river during the waning days of summer. Beginning in early August, the fish congregate offshore from the rivermouths, waiting to start their winter run. If the weather is just right, the sea's surface calm and visibility unhampered by fog, the flashing bodies of thousands of steelhead can be seen just under water. You will glimpse quick darting silver streaks in almost every square yard of the sea as the fish race about, in pursuit of shrimp and other morsels that will cram into their compact, streamlined bodies enough energy to carry them to their spawning grounds and to sustain them until they return to the ocean, weeks or even months later.

From rivermouth to spawning beds may be a journey of only a day or two, but it might be, as is the case of the steelhead returning to such huge rivers as the Columbia, a journey of hundreds of miles and lasting as long as eight months. Steelhead ascending such Columbia River tributaries as the Snake will travel 500 miles inland, and the trip will require almost a year.

Traveling upstream, the steelhead will fight their way through currents and up rapids that often defeat their bigger, stronger cousins, the salmon. Tagging studies have given us a very good idea of the time taken by steelhead on their spawning runs. In the Rogue River of Oregon, an average run of steelhead will travel 60 miles in 21 days, though laggards in the group will approximate the salmon's slower time of 84 days in covering the same distance. In California's Eel River, the average run takes 26 days to cover 65 miles, with slow-moving fish taking up to 61 days.

No similar studies have been made of the movement of steelhead in rivers tributary to the Great Lakes. Such knowledge would be of only academic interest in any event. A large percentage of Great

Lakes tributaries are very short; in Minnesota, for example, many rivers drop over falls within a mile or less of their mouths. Michigan and Wisconsin steelhead streams are often blocked by dams; in such streams a long run for a steelhead migrating upriver would be 30 miles.

In the headwaters of the river, or in one of its tributary creeks, the spawning site the fish will seek is a gravel bed near the center of the stream. Almost invariably, the bed will be at the head of a riffle, at the point where smooth current breaks into white water. The female will not drop her eggs unless her instinct tells her that during low water periods the nesting area will have enough current to aerate the roe until the fry hatch. Once satisfied that her eggs will receive enough oxygen and will not be exposed to air while incubating, the female swims over the nesting area, usually followed by one or more males. Not until she has made a thorough study of the gravel bed will she choose the site for the first of several nests that she will use.

Depending on which point of view you take, the female steelhead is either very liberated or completely male-dominated. It is the female that leads the male to the nesting area, who chooses the best nest site, and, finally, who digs the nest itself. Technically called a redd, the nest is created by the fish hovering on her side and fanning rhythmically with her tail until a pitlike depression four to eight inches deep and a foot in diameter has been scooped out in the coarse gravel. While the female is working, the male hovers nearby, and when at last she moves into position over the nest, he comes alongside her, staying downstream and slightly behind her. In this position the pair will remain for several minutes.

Occasionally, the male will rub the female's body with his nose; he may leave the redd momentarily to chase away a male that has intrided on the nesting territory, but he quickly returns to his mate. For a half hour or longer the pair will hold their position over the nest, an inch or so apart, their bodies quivering from time to time in what must be some sort of sexual excitement, and is often mistaken for the act of mating. It is not, however; the mating is as chaste and disembodied as most fish matings are. The female drops a string of barley-sized roe and at the same time the male discharges a cloud of milt; roe and milt mingle as they float gently down into the waiting nest.

A female does not drop all her eggs at once. A pair of mating steelhead will make five or six nests covering fifteen to twenty square yards of the spawning bed. Each nest will be upstream from the last, the silt and gravel stirred up as the female excavates each new redd washing down to cover the last one. In this series of nests the female will deposit between 7500 and 9500 eggs, depending on her size; a roe-count of over 500 female steelhead ranged from a low of 2400 to a high of 11,000, with the number of eggs in the roe sac varying in direct ratio to the fish's weight and size.

Nest studies show that almost 100 percent of the fertilized eggs will hatch. Covered with four to six inches of gravel to keep them from being gobbled down by other fish, supplied with oxygen by the stream's current, the eggs incubate for 50 to 75 days, depending on water temperature. When the fry emerge, they will be the length of a fingernail, and so small that just over 300 would weigh an ounce. Their first nourishment comes from the egg sacs that remain attached to their bodies. These sacs are almost pure protein and sustain the tiny fish for three to four days, while the fry remain under the gravel in the nest.

By the time the egg sacs are absorbed, the steelhead fry will have gained one-third in weight (they would now weigh 200 to the ounce) and have increased in length to about an inch. They now have the strength to fight their way through the shielding gravel, out of the nest, so the steelhead's life begins as it so often ends—with a struggle.

In their natural environment, only about three percent of the fry grow to maturity; from 7500 eggs, fewer than 200 adult fish will be produced. For two to three weeks, the fry stay in the vicinity of the nest, then they begin to work their way into deeper water. During this period the baby steelhead are vegetarians, eating plankton and algae produced in the moss that covers the rocks on the river bottom. Four to six months after hatching, the exact period depending on water temperature and the quantity of food available, the young steelhead will have grown into what the residents of the area call "half-pounders." It is at this stage in their growth that they are indistinguishable from small rainbow trout; the fish will be eight to twelve inches long and weigh between one-half and three-quarters of a pound. It is also at this stage that the steelhead begin to seek the ocean, moving purposefully downstream into salt water, there to stay until they return for their first spawning run.

A first-year spawner may weigh as little as four pounds or may be twice that heavy; there seems no pattern to be discovered in the size to which a steelhead will grow during its first year in the sea. Lacking knowledge of the fish's movements and habits in the ocean, biologists can only speculate that some of the fish go to areas where food is plentiful and others spend their time in places where less food is available. With each round-trip from sea to spawning bed, of course, the steelhead grows bigger, tougher, better able to do battle, more interesting to the angler.

Just how interesting depends on two factors. One of these, the choice of suitable tackle, the fisherman can control. The second factor is uncontrollable; it is the temperature of the water. By nature the steelhead is a cold-water fish. It fights best when the stream's temperature is within the 42- to 48-degree range; happily, this is the normal winter range of most of the rivers the fish favors. In 50-degree water the steelhead becomes sluggish; in water below 42 degrees it is logy; and it will not survive long if the water it is in drops below 36 degrees.

Because of the fish's sensitivity to temperatures, many veteran steelheaders concentrate on the winter runs. Although summer steelhead will react explosively to the hook's sting on days when the water is just right, the percentage of greatly active fish is far higher during the winter months. This is, of course, angler's choice. Those who are prepared to endure the physical discomforts of winter steelheading will find the rewards greater than those who elect to fish on sunny days in their shirt-sleeves. More will be said about both winter and summer fishing in a later chapter.

Winter or summer, though, in water that pleases him, the steelhead is supreme. The season is less important than the fish; what matters is that at any time the steelhead hits your bait or lure or fly, you will experience such a battle that almost every fish hooked takes on an individuality of its own. This is something unique, something that belongs exclusively to the steelhead: the ability to impress the man who catches it to such an extent that each fish remains an individual memory long after the tackle has been stowed away and the fishing trip ended.

2

Pacific Steelhead

Steelhead country in the West is a relatively narrow strip of the three coastal states starting fifty miles north of San Francisco Bay and running to the Canadian border. With a few exceptions that will be duly noted, the strip goes inland from the ocean from 75 to 100 miles.

Not all the steelhead streams on the continent are within this area, of course. There are fabulous rivers in British Columbia and on up the coastline to the northernmost limits of Alaska, almost to the point where the Arctic icecap imposes its permanent closure on running rivers. Steelhead also enter the Asian rivers that flow through Russia, Manchuria, and Korea down to about the 38th parallel, or approximately as far south as the fish is found in North America.

What Asian streams the steelhead uses are of small interest to anglers; fishermen are among those kept out by the Iron Curtain. And in this book I have not tried to cover the rivers north of the Canadian line, since many of them are hard to reach and have few facilities for travelers. They are there, though, waiting to be explored.

Formed late in history, as geologists measure time, the rivers of the Pacific Northwest rush swiftly from a narrow range of coastal mountains down steep inclines to the sea. For the most part, they are big rivers but short ones; they will drop in a dozen miles altitudes which gentler streams take hundreds of miles to fall. Observed casually, they appear to be turgid, slow-moving streams, but this first impression is deceptive.

These rivers have not yet cut themselves into the deep gorges that will in future centuries allow them to meander lazily to the ocean. A few have eroded the surface soil into steep-walled canyons, but the majority flow between gently sloped banks paved with the same coarse gravel and big rocks that form the river bottoms. Their real power is concealed; only in those places where formations of bed-rock stone thrust up from the streambed can it be seen. In such spots the current sends the water climbing in thick shimmering sheets up the sides of the stones, and where the rocks split the water its surface breaks into a frothing, bubbling, boiling white screen, half-hidden by sprays of foam.

There are a few gentle streams in steelhead country; California's Mattole and Oregon's Tillamook are good examples. But the easy-flowing rivers are far outnumbered by the brawlers, those that are both wide and fast-moving, with heavy currents that create unexpected undertows and gouge deep pockets into the graveled bottoms. In over 300 of the rivers of the northwestern coast, the steelhead make their temporary homes.

Not all the 300 rivers that carry steelhead in Washington, Oregon, and California offer consistent fishing. Fifty of them afford outstanding sport, and of the fifty, ten stand head and shoulders above the rest. But, if a friend tells you about a fabulous steelhead river of which you've never heard before, it's best to believe him until you've tested it yourself. There are many good steelhead streams as yet undiscovered by any but residents of the area through which they flow. No one man has yet fished all the steelhead rivers.

There are streams which have not been publicized because they have few towns along their courses, or because they are only now being reached by easily-traveled access roads. Because the steelhead in fresh water is almost constantly in motion, those who fish for it must be prepared to travel, too. Often a river will be barren at Point A, where you are fishing, but will be thick with steelhead a mile or two upstream or down. This constant movement of the fish makes access roads of great importance; one of the requisites of a good steelhead river is that it can be reached along most of its productive length by a road running parallel.

More and more, the county and state road-building agencies in the three steelhead states are adopting the suggestion of fish and game departments and sportsmen's groups. When a road is built parallel to steelhead water, the road-building agency buys right-of-way to the river, and thus insures the fisherman access to the stream. However, western riparian law does not encourage closed waters. In California and Washington, rivers are open to the public for fishing from water's edge to high-water mark; in the case of big streams, the high-water mark established when the river is in flood may be a half mile from the normal bank. In Oregon, the water itself is open to fishermen wading or in boats. In all three states, if you cannot reach the stream over public land, say from a highway right-of-way or a bridge approach, you must get permission to cross private property to the stream. But in all three states, no landowner can build a fence across a stream.

If you are a stranger in steelhead country, or fishing in an area strange to you, you're well-advised to choose from the better-known rivers. There are reasons justifying their reputations, and along these streams the angler will almost always find accommodations and facilities that make his trip more pleasant as well as access roads that make his fishing easier.

Another bit of advice that veterans will not need, but that novices might find useful, is to keep in mind that size is no criterion of a steelhead river's productivity. A good example is California's Smith

River, which lies between the Klamath and the Rogue. The Smith is barely thirty miles long, but in January and February it produces runs of astonishing size and big, vigorous fish; it also clears faster after a rain than do most neighboring streams and is fishable days before the better-known Rogue and Klamath. In Oregon, the Tillamook is another example of a short, productive, quick-clearing steelhead river. And the Hoh, Quinault, and Sol Duc on Washington's Olympic Peninsula are short in length but long in steelhead productivity.

Although you will find a few steelhead in almost all the rivers that empty into the Pacific north of San Francisco Bay, making a blind choice from among them is not a good idea. As for the rivers south of San Francisco, probably fifteen to twenty will yield an occasional steelhead, usually to local anglers familiar with the pinpoint locations where a fish or two might be found. Runs in these streams are small and inconsistent, and the fishing itself of secondary quality; even in winter these rivers are warm, and the fish sluggish.

When entering unfamiliar areas of steelhead country, it's well to study a map in advance of your trip. Pacific Northwest rivers have peculiarities all their own. Because they are short streams and because rains are sudden and heavy during the best steelhead months, a river will often rise to flood stage overnight, or if it does not flood, it will become so fast and roiled with mud that fishing it is impossible. At the same time, a river ten miles or less away might have escaped the headwaters rain that spoiled the condition of the stream you had planned to fish. So, make your headquarters where you will be able to reach more than one key river; there are so many good streams that this is easy to do with the aid of a map and some advance planning.

Another peculiarity of the West Coast rivers is that they often have sandbars across their mouths, and steelhead will not enter such streams until the bars have washed away. To the angler, this means waiting until after the first big rain has increased the river's flow enough to remove the bar, and then waiting still longer until the water has cleared enough to make fishing feasible. One other characteristic should be noted, and this is the fact that many steelhead streams are backed up by their sand-closed mouths to form tidal or coastal lagoons. These lagoons offer very fine fishing much of the time, and lack the heavy currents that make the upper reaches of the streams so difficult for the novice steelheader to navigate either wading or in a boat.

Not all maps show all the access roads to steelhead rivers, nor do all maps give full information about details such as sandbars and lagoons. Specific information about most rivers can be obtained from state fish and game offices, and from local civic organizations such as Chambers of Commerce and booster clubs in towns near the individual rivers. In many cases, maps showing hot spots will be sent you without charge. If you arrive in a steelhead country town, the hotel or motel clerk, the attendant at the service station, the salesman at the tackle store, will all be ready to help you with directions and advice. And if one of them offers to go along with you on your fishing trip, by all means accept the offer, for he'll know the local water much better than you do.

Now, to get specific. First, to name the ten streams that have by their past records for consistently yielding big fish and producing sport with regularity earned the right to top rank.

Moving north from San Francisco up the coast, the first of these big ten rivers is the Eel, included because it not only produces good fish regularly, but because its current is lighter than most big rivers and the fisherman gets more "feel" of the steelhead he hooks here. A few miles north, the Klamath, a productive stream with a winter season extending from September to January. Above the Klamath, the Rogue, a river that challenges the expert in many stretches but offers opportunity for the novice in its quieter waters; the Rogue's upper reaches accessible from both Medford and Grants Pass provide exceptionally good steelheading.

Moving on north in Oregon, we next come to the Umpqua, and especially its North Fork, famed in recent years as one of the outstanding summer steelhead rivers and offering fine winter fishing as well. The Suislaw is next, and though it does not have the wide acclaim of some of its neighbors, it is a sound and consistently productive river. From here, our next step is to the mighty Columbia, and with this river things begin to get complicated. A fisherman could spend a very full lifetime exploring all the Columbia's tributaries and still miss half the best water. The main Columbia is a difficult river to assess, but among its tributaries are two that must go into the top ten listing. These are the Deschutes, rising in central Oregon and flowing north to join the big river at The Dalles; and the Cowlitz, which rushes through a rich valley to enter the Columbia near Kelso, Washington. Both these come close to qualifying as all-year rivers.

To complete the list, we add the Skykomish, which empties into Puget Sound near Everett, Washington, and is an exceptionally fine river to fish in its upper areas during midwinter; and on the Olympic Peninsula, the Sol Duc, a short stream where the fish are fresh from salt water and filled with vigor. Finally, far to the North, there is the Nooksack, with its mouth near Bellingham, Washington, which is recommended both for the quality of its fishing and the civilized surroundings it offers the angler.

Steelheaders living in the Pacific Northwest will probably want to argue this selection, but the tendency of fishermen to enjoy debate has already been noted, and I'll be the first to admit that there's no statistical justification for my choices. Even if there were figures that could be cited giving the number of fish taken along each yard of each of these streams, and the size of each fish caught, there would be differences of opinion. My choices are based on personal exploration covering a period of many years, discussions with other anglers, and a distillation of such intangibles as the mood of the rivers themselves.

To me, and to others with whom I've compared notes, some streams are friendly and welcoming, while others seem to glower unhappily at the fishermen wandering along its banks or breasting its currents in waders or by boat. I refuse to fish some rivers because their atmosphere doesn't appeal to me. However, I also have learned that what repels me may attract another; while I like my coffee black, I serve cream and sugar to friends who prefer their brew seasoned. So, to a certain extent, my selection of the top ten steelhead rivers is arbitrary insofar as when two streams offer equally good fishing, I've favored the one I enjoy the most.

Like so many other things, fishing is a personal affair, and steelhead fishing very greatly so. I like to try my luck in a number of rivers in the course of a fishing season, yet many of my good angling companions will go to only two or three favorite riffles, perhaps on only one or two streams. These men will cover as little as three or four miles of water between September and January, even though some of them fish almost every day. And, at the end of a season, they will have taken as many fish and as big fish as will the man who visits twenty riffles on a dozen streams and covers a hundred miles of water. If, then, my "top ten" list doesn't include your favorite river, put it down to personal prejudice and look for it in the list of the fifty best steelhead streams that follows.

Again, I make no pretense that the list of fifty is definitive, for it contains only 25 percent to 30 percent of all the steelhead rivers. It is arbitrary in that it starts with the Russian River, just above San Francisco Bay, and ends at the Canadian border; this geographical limitation is self-imposed. There are also some interior rivers that have been omitted from the list. One is the Snake, the other the Sacramento, to mention the principal omissions. The Snake and its tributaries in Washington and Idaho share the Columbia River runs and carry fish to their spawning beds almost a thousand miles from salt water. The Sacramento—and to a lesser extent the San Joaquin River south of it—hold winter steelhead, often big ones.

These inland rivers have been left off intentionally, not overlooked by accident. As good as the fishing is in certain limited areas along them, these areas are limited in extent and irregular as to season. The fisherman looking for consistent, easily found steelhead fishing is better off confining his activities to the coastal streams. And certainly on the list of fifty or so streams that follows, even the most active angler will find enough good water to keep him busy indefinitely.

One explanatory note: in the right-hand column of the list, under the heading "Best Months and Other Data," mention is made of accommodations and facilities. To give you a consistent frame of reference, "Good" accommodations means that you have a choice ranging from the luxurious to the primitive; "Limited" refers to both quality and quantity; you might not be able to find rooms with private baths close to the stream and in peak months should reserve far in advance; "Very Limited" means you should expect nothing beyond a roof, bare walls, and a bedstead and would probably be better off taking a tent or traveling in a camper-type vehicle. As used on the list, "Facilities" covers restaurants, tackle shops, boat rentals, guides, and so on. Remember, too, that conditions change, and to be absolutely safe, call or write in advance before making plans.

River	State	Highway Access	Nearest Town	Best Months & Other Data
Alsea	Oregon	U.S. 101	Waldport	Nov.-Feb. State 34 parallels river but has no accommodations between Waldport and Corvallis; facilities very limited.
Albion	California	State 1	Ft. Bragg	Dec.-Jan. Best fishing at tidewater from boats; no boat rentals, so bring your own. Limited accommodations and facilities except at Ft. Bragg where both are good.
Chetco	Oregon	U.S. 101	Brookings	Jan.-Feb. Good in cycles of two years; find out before going how cycle is running. Good accommodations and facilities.
Cowlitz	Washington	U.S. 99	Kelso	Jan.-Mar. One of the big rivers. State 5 takes you to most of the upper water. Good accommodations and facilities along most of river.

Columbia	Washington Oregon	U.S. 99-101 U.S. 30-830		A lifetime project. There are scores of tributaries and dozens of towns along U.S. 830 on the north bank and U.S. 30 on the south bank from which most tributaries can be reached via good access roads. From Portland to the mouth of the Umatilla, take your choice; the best tributary streams are on this list, but it's impossible to include all.
Coos	Oregon	U.S. 101	Coos Bay	Nov.-Jan. From Dellwood, where boats and guides available, a county road gives access to lower river. Good accommodations and facilities.
Coquille	Oregon	U.S. 101	Bandon	Nov.-Jan. From Bandon to Coquille U.S. 102 parallels river, giving access to the South Fork. At road-end, Agness is starting point for south Rogue Gorge. Outside Bandon accommodations and facilities limited.

River	State	Highway Access	Nearest Town	Best Months & Other Data
Deschutes	Oregon	U.S. 30	Miller	Nov.-Jan. Access to most of river via county road from Miller, but outside Miller accommodations and facilities very limited.
Dosewallips	Washington	U.S. 101	Brinnon	Dec.-Feb. Limited accommodations at Brinnon and very limited along river.
Duckabush	Washington	U.S. 101	Brinnon	Nov.-Feb. Also a good run of summer steelhead beginning late May. Outside Brinnon, very limited accommodations.
Dungeness	Washington	U.S. 101	Sequim	Dec.-Feb. Rainwear very necessary. Limited accommodations and facilities.
Eel	California	U.S. 101	Fortuna (lower) Garberville (upper)	Oct.-Jan. Or, until big rains begin; be sure to check local weather. Top fly fishing when water is clear. Boat needed to fish big water at mouth, boats available at Loleta. Eel South Fork accessible via county road from Weott, also good. Lower river accommodations good, upper river limited.

Garcia	California	State 1	Pt. Arena	December. Best at tidewater but a few good riffles upstream; very lightly fished. Limited accommodations and facilities.
Green	Washington	U.S. 99	Seattle (lower) Palmer (upper)	Jan.-Feb. Very heavy fishing pressure, especially in lower river areas. A highly civilized stream; good accommodations and facilities.
Gualala	California	State 1	Gualala	Dec.-Jan. Open only after heavy rains wash out bar at mouth; inquire before going. Limited accommodations.
Hoh	Washington	U.S. 101	Hoh	Dec.-Feb. As on most rivers of Olympic Peninsula, very light fishing pressure. Parallel access road gets rough at times but passable. Limited accommodations.
Humptulips	Washington	U.S. 101	Humptulips	Dec.-Feb. Rainwear a must during season on Olympic Peninsula rivers. Lightly fished, limited accommodations and facilities.

River	State	Highway Access	Nearest Town	Best Months & Other Data
Kalama	Washington	U.S. 99	Kalama	March-April. Try upstream at Pigeon Springs area, where boats and guides available. Good accommodations and facilities.
Klamath	California	U.S. 101 State 96	Klamath (lower) Orleans, Happy Camp (upper)	Sept.-Feb., but October-November peak months. Lower river best fished from boats, no access roads from 8 miles above mouth to 30 miles upstream. Boats and guides at Klamath. Upper river best fished wading; fly fishing superior. Good accommodations for lower river; limited at Orleans and Weitchipec for central stream and at Happy Camp for upper.
Klickitat	Washington	U.S. 830	Lyle	Nov.-Feb. Also fine summer fishing, May-July. Good accommodations and facilities.
Lewis	Washington	U.S. 99	Woodland	Jan.-Mar. Best in short stretches below dams. Good accommodations and facilities.

Mad	California	U.S. 101	Arcata	Nov.-Feb. Lower river near tidewater best. No boats or guides, good accommodations. U.S. 299 gives access to upper river.
Mattole	California	State 36	Petrolia	Dec.-Jan. Bar must be washed out before fish will enter river. Small stream, lightly fished. No accommodations near river.
Necanium	Oregon	U.S. 101	Seaside	Dec.-Feb. Good accommodations and facilities for lower river, none upstream.
Nehalem	Oregon	U.S. 101	Mohler	Dec.-Feb. A short but very active stream. Good accommodations and facilities.
Nestucca	Oregon	U.S. 101	Cloverdale	Dec.-Feb. Try tidewater around Pacific City. Good accommodations and facilities.
Nooksack	Washington	U.S. 99	Bellingham	Jan.-Mar. Crowded in downstream areas; for solitude try North and South Forks, reached from Deming via State 1. While in this area, a worthwhile sidetrip is one to the Fraser River just a few miles north in British Columbia. Good accommodations.

River	State	Highway Access	Nearest Town	Best Months & Other Data
Navarro	California	State 1	Ft. Bragg	Dec.-Jan. Lagoon and tidewater best, a few boats available. Good—and only—accommodations are at Ft. Bragg, none closer to river.
Noyo	California	State 1	Ft. Bragg	Dec.-Jan. Same story as Navarro, above.
Puyallup	Washington	U.S. 99	Tacoma	Feb.-Mar. Heavily fished near city; go upstream via State 5 to Orting and choose either Upper Puyallup or nearby Carbon River. Both streams good, with good accommodations and facilities.
Queets	Washington	U.S. 99	Queets	Nov.-Feb. Also close by is Clearwater River. Adequate accommodations.
Quinault	Washington	U.S. 101 State 9C	Taholah	Nov.-Feb. Best bet: try at Lake Quinault for guides and fish from lake as headquarters. A summer run in mid-July. Good accommodations.
Redwood Creek	California	U.S. 101	Orick	Jan.-Feb. Don't let the word "creek" fool you; it's a good big stream, if short. Big runs and big fish; work upstream beyond channelized banks. Adequate accommodations and facilities.

Rogue	Oregon	U.S. 99	Grants Pass Medford (upper)	Sept.-Mar. As good as any river you'll find, better than
		U.S. 101	Gold Beach (lower)	most. Best fished from boat, both boats and guides available at Grants Pass, Medford, Gold Beach. Upper river towns have good accommodations and facilities; those for lower river limited. Try taking the mail-boat from Gold Beach to Agness, stay overnight there and fish middle river wading. Or, boat will drop you anywhere along stream you want to camp, pick you up when you specify. Good summer run, July. Advance reservations for boats, guides, or in lower river area, accommodations, an absolute must.
Russian	California	U.S. 101	Healdsburg (upper)	Dec.-Jan. Heavy fishing pressure all along
		State 1	Jenner (lower)	river; boat is best bet, both boats and guides readily available. Good accommodations and facilities everywhere along stream, but reserve well in advance.

River	State	Highway Access	Nearest Town	Best Months & Other Data
Siletz	Oregon	U.S. 101	Kernville	Nov.-Feb. While in area, try also the Yaquina and Elk, both close by. Good accommodations and facilities.
Skagit	Washington	U.S. 99	Mt. Vernon	Feb.-Mar. For upper river, take State 17 to Lyman, where guides and boats available. Good accommodations and facilities.
Skykomish	Washington	U.S. 99	Everett	Dec.-Jan. Lower river heavily fished; less pressure upstream. Take State 17 to Gold Bar or Startup. Good accommodations and facilities.
Sixes	Oregon	U.S. 101	Sixes	Nov.-Jan. Short stream, very active, little fishing pressure. Limited accommodations and facilities.
Smith	California	U.S. 101	Crescent City	Jan.-Feb. At mouth, good fishing and accommodations, very limited upstream where fishing equally good. Boats and guides available. Crescent City and at one or two mid-river resorts. Reserve.

Smiths	Oregon	U.S. 101	Reedsport	Nov.-Jan. Easily accessible. Small summer run, June-July. Limited accommodations and facilities.
Snake	Washington	U.S. 410	Pasco	March-April. Listing is for lower river only, a predictably good stream in Pasco area, spotty upstream. Good accommodations and facilities.
Sol Duc	Washington	U.S. 101	Forks	Dec.-Feb. One of the very good streams. Also try the Bogachiel and Calawah near by. Take rainwear. Good accommodations and facilities.
Stillagaumish	Washington	U.S. 101	Arlington	Jan.-Feb. Most of river readily available via State 1A, 1E, and 15A. Summer run, July-August. Good accommodations and facilities.
Suislaw	Oregon	U.S. 101	Florence	Dec.-Jan. State 36 gives access to most of stream. Good accommodations but limited facilities; be ready to eat picnic-style.

River	State	Highway Access	Nearest Town	Best Months & Other Data
Tillamook	Oregon	U.S. 101	Tillamook	Nov.-Jan. Short, shallow, easily-fished stream. Good fly water. Also try bigger rivers, Trask and Wilson, both accessible via county roads from Tillamook, where accommodations and facilities good. Boats, guides, available at Tillamook.
Trinity	California	U.S. 299	Willow Creek	Nov.-Jan. Get a guide from Hoopa Indian reservation through which best fishing water flows; avoid Indian lands unless you have guide, go upstream to Solyer. Limited accommodations and facilities.
Upmqua	Oregon	U.S. 99 U.S. 101	Roseburg (upper) Reedsport (lower)	Nov.-Feb. in lower river, Dec.-Mar. in upper. North Fork especially good. A big summer steelhead river, runs late June to early August. Wadable most places. Good accommodations and facilities.

Van Duzen	California	U.S. 101	Fortuna (lower)	Dec.-Feb. Access limited to bridge approaches and in upper river to county roads. Good accommodations lower, none upper.
		State 36	Bridgeville (upper)	
Washougal	Washington	U.S. 830	Washougal	Feb.-Mar. Excellent late-season runs. Good accommodations and facilities.
Wilson	Oregon	U.S. 101	Tillamook	Dec.-Jan. Best near mouth, close to tidewater, but good access via county roads enables angler to follow runs upstream. Accommodations only in tillamook, good.
Wind	Washington	U.S. 830	Carson	Feb.-Mar. Go north on State 8C paralleling river, to Mineral Springs. Good accommodations and facilities.
Yaquina	Oregon	U.S. 101	Newport	Nov.-Jan. Two other good streams nearby are Elk and Siletz. Good accommodations and facilities.

As all anglers know, the character of a stream undergoes changes from year to year. Strangely, in spite of their habit of flooding heavily and regularly, steelhead rivers stay remarkably consistent. Those listed on the foregoing pages have been furnishing sport for decades, and most have improved in recent years. Quite equally, the character of the land around the streams, and the access roads as well, weill change; the roads faster than anything else. Always make local inquiry to find out if roads have been renumbered. And, when planning to go to a popular stream such as the Rogue, reserve everything well in advance.

Migrating steelhead on the Umpqua in Oregon, photographed in a glass-walled observation chamber at the Winchester Counting Station. Above, a male steelhead ready to spawn. Below, a female. Photos by Jerry Bauer, courtesy Oregon State Game Commission.

At Gravel Pit Riffle on Oregon's Kilchis River, Al Mills of Bay City brings a steelhead back after its first downstream dash. Tail-dancing, the fish shows it's not quite ready to be beached.

A final desperation dash and a last jump as Al backs out of the water, and the steelhead is ready to come in. The reward: eight pounds of gleaming fresh-run winter fish.

A drift boat follows a jumping steelhead down the Wilson River in northern Oregon.

A drift boat about to enter Hell Gate in the Rogue River Gorge, Oregon. This stretch is notorious for chewing up boats.

Drifting the Suislaw through early-morning mist, a pair of anglers take an active steelhead.

It takes a light, delicate hand to lead the tired fish to
the boat.

A swoop of the net, and the fish is safe. Photographed on the North
Umpqua by Pete Cornachia.

In Lake Muskegon, Michigan, a trolled wabbling lure brings a steelhead to boat. Photo courtesy *Muskegon Chronicle*.

Midwestern steelhead are well fed and run large. Michigan's Big Manistee yielded this 17-pounder to Fred Rochyk of Joliet, Ill. Photo by Ralph Fairbanks.

What the well-dressed winter steelheader will wear. This is the upper Eel in California. Photo by Irv Urie.

3

Great Lakes Steelhead

In the Great Lakes region, steelhead country spreads over a much wider chunk of geography than on the Pacific Coast, though again the steelhead's domain comprises only three states. Starting at Saginaw Bay on the eastern side of Michigan's Lower Peninsula, steelhead rivers flow east into Lake Huron at intervals all the way north to Mackinac Straits, and then continue down the peninsula's Lake Michigan shoreline to a point fifty miles south of Muskegon. In the state's Upper Peninsula, steelhead streams begin just west of Whitefish Bay on the peninsula's northern side and extend west and north along the Lake Superior watersheds of Michigan, Wisconsin, and Minnesota. Then, returning south to Wisconsin's Lake Michigan shoreline, steelhead rivers will be found from the tip of the Potawatomi Peninsula down to Sheboygan.

This is a lot of territory, and it includes literally hundreds of rivers. Not all of the streams attract steelhead, although in most of them an occasional straying explorer fish will be picked up. There are perhaps sixty rivers in the three Great Lakes states that are good steelhead streams, and half of these can be classed as excellent, using the criteria of dependability and size of the steelhead runs. Of the thirty excellent streams, a dozen are outstanding; these rivers will meet the tests of dependability and regularity of runs and numbers and size of fish. And the Great Lakes steelhead region offers a rivermouth and offshore fishery that has no parallel in the west.

Rivers of inland steelhead country tend to be smaller, tamer, and usually shorter than Pacific Coast streams. This is a boon to the fisherman, for he has fewer miles per stream to explore before finding good fishing, and in those rivers chosen by the steelhead for their spawning runs the ratio of fish to water area is much higher, the fish concentration greater. Stream size, as was noted earlier, seems to make little difference to the steelhead, and those that swim up the smoother, gentler currents of Great Lakes rivers are as big, as lusty and brawling, and as challenging to the angler as are their ancestors in the wider, swifter waters of the Pacific Coast.

The steelhead is not native to the Great Lakes watershed, but the fish was introduced enough years ago to give today's steelhead the status of respected pioneers, if not natives. Michigan's fishery biologists imported the first eggs from "wild Oregon steelhead" in the 1870s. This was an experiment, to find out whether the fish would adapt to a totally freshwater environment, whether they would migrate into the Great Lakes as they do into the ocean, and whether they would return to the rivers to spawn.

Happily, the steelhead proved adaptable. Fish hatched from the Oregon steelhead eggs and planted in Michigan streams behaved just as they would have in far western waters. They entered Lake Michigan and Lake Huron as smolts, lived a year or two or three in the big lakes, returned to the rivers, spawned, multiplied, and thrived.

Steelhead fishing flourished in Michigan streams until the proliferation of dams across the lower reaches of the rivers denied the fish access to their spawning beds. Natural reproduction diminished in the years that followed the area's industrial expansion beginning in the early 1900s and peaking in the boom after World War I. In the meantime, though, the steelhead had traveled widely. Some crossed Lake Michigan to find new spawning beds in Wisconsin rivers and in the streams of Michigan's Upper Peninsula. Others migrated east through the Straits of Mackinac and joined journeying Lake Huron steelhead to travel through the narrows at Sault Ste. Marie and into Lake Superior. These fish established themselves in small numbers in the Superior watershed streams of Michigan's Upper Peninsula, Wisconsin, and Minnesota.

There were never enough of these far-ranging migrants to establish the steelhead as a major fish in the Lake Superior tributaries. Among the then-plentiful lake trout and native stream trout their presence went virtually unnoticed. All three of the Great Lakes states had introduced western rainbow trout into their waters long before Michigan's steelhead experiment, and anglers of the early days failed to distinguish between the steelhead and the rainbows. It was not until the sea lamprey invaded the Great Lakes in the early 1930s that the steelhead began to be looked at with more than casual interest, and as a species different from the rainbow.

A digression is in order at this point. To understand the resurgence of steelhead in the Great Lakes watershed after the 1970s, it is necessary that we look at the lamprey-alewife-steelhead biological chain. The story is one of interest not only to steelhead fishermen, but to all who pay attention to our environment. It is an example of the way that man can bring about the virtual extinction of fish in formerly productive waters by thoughtless "improvements," and how he can then remedy the damage his tinkering has caused.

In 1932, the Welland Canal that bypasses Niagara Falls and provides a channel for oceangoing ships was opened between Lake Ontario and Lake Erie. The canal, located in Canada at the northwestern tip of New York State, replaced an earlier, inadequate, century-old water link. Designed to give deep-water shipping easy access to the important industrial areas that dot the borders of

Lakes Erie, Huron, Michigan, and Superior, the canal also did something that its builders had not planned: it opened those lakes to the invasion of two species of marine life that virtually destroyed the food and sport fish that hitherto had lived in Great Lakes waters.

These two invaders were the sea lamprey and the alewife. Both are anadromous fish, dividing their time between fresh and salt water. Both found a rich source of food in the huge expanses of the Great Lakes, and both lampreys and alewives took up permanent residence in their waters and multiplied explosively as a result of the new food supply. The lamprey is parasitic; it preys on large fish, attaching itself to their bellies or sides with a serrated sucker-mouth and draining their lives away. The alewife gorges on the eggs and fry of other fish.

Within ten years after the opening of the Welland Canal, the food and sport fish population of Lake Huron and Lake Michigan began a precipitous decline, and within the next few years a similar decline could be seen in Lake Superior. By the middle of the 1950s, the lake trout, whitefish, walleye, and yellow perch—predators as well as food and sport fish species—were beginning to go at an accelerated rate, and by the end of the 1950s these species had almost vanished. The lamprey took its toll of mature fish, which reduced the numbers available for reproduction, while the burgeoning alewife population wiped the spawning areas clean of eggs and fry.

Trash fish, formerly kept in check by the bigger predator fish, multipled enormously as the number of predator fish dwindled. By the start of the 1960s, the number of trash fish—chubs, minnows, alewives—had grown so large that even the Great Lakes could not produce enough of the plankton, algae, marine insect life, fish roe and fry that provided food for the trash fish. By the hundreds of thousands they died—the alewife dying in the most prodigious numbers—and their bodies washed ashore on the beaches, creating a massive disposal problem and presenting a potential source of water pollution. Both sport and food fishing in the Great Lakes seemed to be at an end.

Biologists had foreseen that this would happen, and as early as the mid-1940s a crash program was begun to find a selective poison that would work on the sea lamprey and leave other fish unharmed. Such a poison was discovered by the mid-1950s, and the lamprey began to be brought under control. By then, however, mature predator fish had died in such great numbers that not enough were left to reduce the billions of alewives that by then inhabited the lakes. Nor could the predator fish multiply adequately, for they spawn in the lakes and their eggs and fry were consumed to near totality by the vastly more numerous alewives.

Only one fish of the Great Lakes was invulnerable to the alewife hordes. This was the steelhead, which spawns in rivers that the alewife does not ascend; additionally, before young steelhead return to the lakes they have grown too large for the alewife to attack. In fact, when steelhead smolts migrate from the streams to the big waters they are already of a size that enables them to prey on the alewife. For the first time in many years, the steelhead began to receive primary consideration from the fish biologists.

Again it was the state of Michigan that took the lead, reviving the steelhead by extensive plantings and at the same time introducing two other anadromous fish that share some of the steelhead's characteristics, the coho and chinook salmon. An experimental planting of 182,000 steelhead fry was made in Michigan streams in 1966, the fry coming from eggs supplied by Oregon and Alaska. At the same time, coho and chinook were planted in much greater numbers; the steelhead's ability to adapt to the Great Lakes environment was known, while the adaptability of salmon to the new habitat was then an unknown quantity. All three species did so well that by 1972 Michigan was planting over a million steelhead eggs annually and had built a major new hatchery on the Platte River near Traverse City that produced more than a million steelhead fry each year, using eggs stripped from fish taken at weirs on several of the state's more productive steelhead streams.

In the Great Lakes today, not only steelhead but lake trout, coho, and chinook salmon are being taken in huge numbers by happy anglers. The sea lamprey is gone, the alewife explosion dampened, as more and more predator fish grow to maturity. To give the steelhead all the credit for this ecological reversal would, of course, be an exaggeration. The fish does get credit for one thing: showing the way. Even for this limited role, steelhead fisherman can be grateful, since in its generally protected Great Lakes habitat, where it is one of the fish at the top of the marine food chain, the steelhead grows big and lusty, fat from a plentiful diet, and returns to the streams in numbers that would have been classed impossible a decade earlier.

Creel surveys of both resident and out-of-state fishermen seeking steelhead in Michigan's waters show that in 1970, only four years after the first fry were planted, sport anglers took 400,000 steelhead from the state's streams and from Lake Michigan. In 1971 a similar survey showed that the number of fish caught increased almost 45 percent in a single year, to nearly 600,000. More than half the steelhead were taken from streams, the remainder being hooked and landed in offshore waters.

Minnesota and Wisconsin began to pay attention to the steelhead later than did Michigan. In early days, as has been shown, these states profited by Michigan's plantings. With the beginning of efforts to revive the Great Lakes fishery, both Minnesota and Wisconsin started steelhead planting programs, but the results of the plantings have been spotty. In many cases the numbers of spawners returning to streams where plants were made has been low, though repeated annual planting is steadily increasing the number of spawning fish that return to the rivers of these two states.

Fishery biologists in both Minnesota and Wisconsin report that steelhead planted in Lake Superior tributaries tend to migrate eastward, into Lake Michigan and in some instances to Lake Huron. Tagged and fin-clipped fish from these two states, taken in Michigan waters, confirm this tendency of steelhead to drift eastward in their big-water wanderings. It can be speculated that this is caused by some vestigial instinct left there from the time when the steelhead in their native habitat knew no other direction except east in which they could migrate. However, enough spawners stay in Lake Superior and return to Minnesota and Wisconsin rivers for the steelhead to be well established in those states, and indications are their numbers will increase.

Food in abundance may be one of the reasons why Lake Superior steelhead travel to Lake Michigan, for in the latter the supply of alewives is far greater. That the Great Lakes steelhead feed voraciously on the alewife is evidenced by their size and fast growth. The Great Lakes fish display a substantially greater body depth and girth than do Pacific Coast steelhead, with a consequent increase in their weight-to-length ratio. Averages are difficult to establish from simple observation, and as yet no scientific studies have been made of size differences between fish of the Great Lakes and those of the Pacific Coast. Until such detailed studies are made, empiricism must serve.

My personal observation, having seen and weighed a substantial number of Western steelhead over the years and after watching the weighing and measuring of over 200 fish at Michigan's Little Manistee weir station late in 1972, is that there is a difference of as much as 12 to 18 percent in the weight-to-length ratio between Pacific Coast and Great Lakes steelhead. A 30-inch male from a far west river can be counted on to tip the scale at 10 to 11 pounds, while a male of this length from a Great Lakes tributary will weigh 12 to 13 pounds. The disparity will be less in small fish and in very big fish, and females heavy with roe will usually outweigh males of equal length by a few ounces.

In part, the greater average weight-to-length ratio of the inland fish can be accounted for by the difference in their diet. Steelhead in the ocean will find generally leaner forage fish than the alewife, which is the predominant diet of Great Lakes steelhead. In addition, the oceangoing fish must work harder, swim farther and faster, for each ounce of food it eats. A third factor has already been mentioned: in the Great Lakes the steelhead is one of the fish at the top of the natural food chain; there are no predators higher on the chain in inland waters. The oceangoing steelhead, though, is about midway in the food chain of the seas. Above it are barracuda, sharks, dogfish, sealions, and many other predators that look on the steelhead as food. In the Pacific, the steelhead keeps lean because it must swim fast and maneuver swiftly just to stay alive.

From the standpoint of the angler, though, steelhead are steelhead wherever they are found. Those in the waters of Michigan, Minnesota, and Wisconsin are taken by the same angling techniques, using the same natural baits, the same lures, and the same flies that bring response from Pacific Coast fish. There are minor differences in equipment and tackle needs, but these are of small importance; where differences do exist they will be noted later in chapters dealing with steelhead fishing methods.

Two things are provided by the Great Lakes area that cannot be matched in western steelhead country. One is the offshore and quiet-water fishery, the other is reliable spring and summer steelheading.

As remarked in an earlier chapter, only one instance has been recorded of a steelhead being caught with hook and line in the Pacific Ocean. In the Great Lakes area, the number of fish taken offshore in Lake Michigan and Lake Superior will usually equal or even exceed the number of fish caught in streams. Few of the dependable western steelhead rivers terminate in quiet-water bays, lakes or lagoons; a relatively large number of the good Great Lakes streams do have such quiet-water pools at their mouths, and in these the fish hang before moving upstream.

Steelhead going up the western rivers to spawn move with determined haste from ocean to spawning bed; the Great Lakes fish do not seem to have this frantic urge to drive on upstream. They hang offshore, and in the lakes and lagoons and bays at rivermouths, and here anglers still-fishing with natural baits or trolling from boats take good harvests of steelhead in both spring and fall.

Even more important than the offshore and rivermouth fishery, however, is the spring and summer steelheading the Great Lakes region offers. At the beginning of spring in this area the streams are usually on the low side with the flow reduced in volume, and the water generally clear. The temperature of the air is moderate, and anglers who have no taste for the rigors of cold weather that winter steelheaders must face can look to the stream and offshore fishing of the Great Lakes for outstanding—and comfortable—sport.

From March through early June, Michigan waters afford excellent steelhead fishing. In Minnesota, late May through mid-July are the best times to fish the rivers or offshore. Wisconsin steelhead fishing begins in May and lasts until midsummer's high temperatures arrive, though in the northern area along Lake Superior fishing continues through the summer, peaking in some streams in July and August. Offshore and rivermouth lake-fishing is usually a bit in advance of the stream peaks in all areas.

While many steelheaders—myself among them—hold to the conviction that the winter steelhead is a tougher, more challenging fish, the spring-run steelhead of the Great Lakes, taken before the waters begin to warm up, are, like all steelhead at almost any season, thoroughly rewarding fish to hook and fight. Fish from such streams as the Bois Brule in northern Wisconsin, the Reservation in upper Minnesota, and the Big Manistee or upper Muskegon in Michigan perform with equal vigor most of the year.

We come now to being specific about the rivers of Great Lakes steelhead country. Identifying the most reliable streams here is a bit more difficult than in the west, where records go back over a long period of years. Because the resurgence of Great Lakes steelheading antedates this writing by such a short span of time it is quite possible that some notable streams of today and of the future are being overlooked. This, of course, is a challenge to you as a fisherman: to find these sleeper rivers and share the knowledge you acquire with other anglers.

It's always dangerous to generalize about rivers and fish, but often generalities are the only solution to keeping information concise. However, you will find in general that the streams of Minnesota are rather short, due to a geological fault that creates impassable falls and steep rapids near the mouths of many rivers. You will also find some of the state's best steelhead fishing in these short streams, and in the rivers that flow through the Finalnd, Pat Bayle, and Grand Portage State Forests and the Superior National Forest. These areas have also been spared overdevelopment, so be prepared to camp or to put up in stripped-down accommodations in areas where the fishing is best. And be prepared, too, for cold weather in early spring and fall.

Wilderness also characterizes the Wisconsin and Michigan rivers that flow into Lake Superior. Here, too, you should not expect luxury accommodations close to the streams. The Lake Michigan rivers of Wisconsin flow through a more settled countryside, while the Michigan streams in the Lower Peninsula also traverse a more populous area. In these places you will find good accommodations and such services as rental and charter boats and guides around most of the better-known, most productive rivers and offshore fishing spots.

By states, then, the Michigan rivers that merit your close attention are the Two Hearted River and the Little Garlic River in the Upper Peninsula, the Muskegon, Big Manistee, and Pere Marquette on the Lower Peninsula's Lake Michigan side, and the AuGres on the Huron side. In Minnesota, the Knife, Devil's Track and Reservation Rivers are among the most dependable. The Knife and Nemadji—the latter flowing through both Minnesota and Wisconsin—are Minnesota's largest steelhead streams. In Wisconsin, try the Bois Brule (usually called the Brule, but given its full name here to distinguish it from a stream of the same name in Minnesota) and the Sioux on the Lake Superior watershed, and on the Lake Michigan side to the Kewaunee and Sheboygan. And do not overlook the shorelines on either side of the mouths of those streams named above and in the list that follows.

Stream fishermen in Great Lakes states must observe one caution that is not required on western rivers, where public access is permitted to high-water mark. In the inland states, property rights go to the water's edge. You can bank-fish without permission if you are standing in the stream itself, or you can wade or fish from a boat in any water, including that fronted by private land. Much privately owned stream frontage is fenced to the water's edge, and usually in such places signs are posted warning against trespass. You must have the property owner's permission to cross fenced, posted land or to fish from the bank rather than standing in the stream.

Now, to give you a consistent frame of reference in the following list of about 30 of the most dependable steelhead rivers of the Great Lakes region, "Good" in the column of comment means that you have a choice of accommodations ranging from luxurious to adequate within a reasonable distance of the stream; "Limited" refers to both quality and availability and means that you might not find rooms with private baths close to the river and should reserve well in advance; "Very Limited" means that you should expect little more than a roof and four walls. "Facilities" includes restaurants, stores, tackle shops, boat rental, charter boats and guide services. Remember, too, that areas change, facilities improve. But, to be safe, inquire and reserve in advance of your trip.

River	*State*	*Highway Access*	*Nearest Town*	*Best Months & Other Data*
Algoma	Wisconsin	State 42 State 54	Algoma	April-May. Good accommodations and facilities at Algoma, limited in upper river area.
AuGres	Michigan	U.S. 23 State 65	AuGres	May-June; Oct.-Nov. Good accommodations and facilities near lower river; upstream is accessible by State 65 through Whitmore, then county roads via Delano and Santiago; best bet upriver is East (Whitney) Branch, access via National City. Upper river accommodations and facilities very limited. Fish offshore in Saginaw Bay, from bank or boat, boats available at AuGres.
Baptism	Minnesota	U.S. 61 to State 1	Silver Bay	May-July. Limited accommodations and facilities along both access roads, but stream access good in state park.

River	State	Highway Access	Nearest Town	Best Months & Other Data
Bear Creek	Michigan	U.S. 31	Manistee	April-May; Nov. Good accommodations and facilities at Manistee, limited at Bretheren and Kaleva. This tributary to the Big Manistee very good and usually dependable.
Betsie	Michigan	U.S. 31 State 115	Beulah	April-June; Nov. Limited accommodations and facilities at Beulah, also at Thomsonville on upper river. Fish lower stream from Freeport, where accommodations and facilities good.
Big Manistee	Michigan	U.S. 31 State 55	Manistee Wellston	April-June; Nov.-Dec. Primarily a boat river but some bank fishing in 3-mile stretch below Tippy Dam. Good accommodations and facilities at both Manistee and Wellston; also fish Manistee Lake and offshore.

Boardman	Michigan	U.S. 31	Traverse City	April-June; Nov.-Dec. Fish below dam near mouth, in East and West arms Grand Traverse Bay; fish from bank, boat. Good accommodations, facilities.
Bois Brule	Wisconsin	U.S. 2	Brule	May-June; Oct. Most of stream readily accessible by unimproved road, trail. Limited accommodations and facilities.
Brule	Minnesota	U.S. 61	Grand Marais	June-August. Good accommodations and facilities at Grand Marais and resorts in area, campsites along stream.
Cascade	Minnesota	U.S. 61	Grand Marais	June-August. Fish river below Deer Yard Lake. Good accommodations and facilities at Grand Marais, resorts along highway.
Devil's Track	Minnesota	U.S. 61	Grand Marais	June-August. Good accommodations and facilities at Grand Marais and resorts along highway, limited at Coltville.

River	State	Highway Access	Nearest Town	Best Months & Other Data
Falls	Michigan	U.S. 41	L'Anse	June-July; Sept.-Nov. Limited accommodations and facilities at L'Anse, very limited upriver. Fish Keeweenaw Bay at rivermouth from bank, boat.
Fish Creek	Wisconsin	State 42	Fish Creek	May-June; Sept.-Oct. Limited accommodations and facilities. Fish bay on both sides of rivermouth from bank, boat.
Huron	Michigan	U.S. 41	L'Anse	June-July; Sept.-Nov. Limited accommodations and facilities at L'Anse and Skanee; access to Skanee via county road which also gives stream access.
Kewaunee	Wisconsin	State 42	Kewaunee	April-May; Oct. Good accommodations and facilities for lower river and offshore fishing at Kewaunee; upriver access by State 54 via Casco and county road via Ellisville; limited accommodations and facilities in upper area.

Knife	Minnesota	U.S. 61	Two Harbors	May-Aug. Limited accommodations and facilities at Two Harbors, very limited at Palmers, Knife River, and Larsmont, where off-shore fishing very good.
Little Garlic	Michigan	U.S. 41	Marquette	May-July; Oct. Stream access via county road from Marquette, where accommodations and facilities good. Very limited accommodations and facilities near river, which is very fine and productive stream.
Little Manistee	Michigan	U.S. 31	Manistee	April-May; Nov.-Dec. Suggest missing this one in spring because of heavy pressure. Less crowded in fall. Good accommodations and facilities at Manistee, limited in upper reaches of river, accessible via county roads off State 51.

River	State	Highway Access	Nearest Town	Best Months & Other Data
Muskegon	Michigan	U.S. 31 U.S. 96	Muskegon	April-June; Oct.-Dec. One of the very productive and dependable streams. Lower river best fished from boat; bank fishing and wading above Newaygo, access via State 46, 37, 82. Take county road to Croton Dam, good fly water for 3 to 4 miles below dam. Accommodations and facilities good, Muskegon and Newaygo, very limited above Newaygo. Also fish Lake Muskegon and bog-area of river-mouth; offshore fish from bank, piers, boat.
Nemadji	Wisconsin Minnesota	State 35 State 23	Superior Duluth	May-June, Sept.-Oct. A two-state river; good runs in water SW of Superior and upstream into Minnesota section. Good accommodations and facilities along most of river in both states.

Pentwater	Michigan	U.S. 31	Hart	April-June; Nov.-Dec. Middle and upper river access via county roads from Hart; lower stream, lake, offshore from Pentwater. Accommodations and facilities limited both Hart and Pentwater.
Pere Marquette	Michigan	U.S. 31 U.S. 10	Ludington Baldwin	April-June; Oct.-Dec. Lower river and lake best fished from boat, available Ludington, where accommodations and facilities good. Upper river access via U.S. 10, State 37, and county roads from Baldwin, Scottville, Custer, Branch; 10 miles of river above Baldwin reserved for fly fishing only. An outstanding stream.
Platte	Michigan	U.S. 31	Honor	April-May; Oct.-Nov. Short but productive stream. Be sure to fish lake at mouth. Limited facilities and accommodations.

River	State	Highway Access	Nearest Town	Best Months & Other Data
Reservation	Minnesota	U.S. 61	Grand Portage	July-August. Limited accommodations at Grand Portage, but resorts along highway provide a range of choices.
Sheboygan	Wisconsin	U.S. 141	Sheboygan	April-June; Sept.-Oct. Short stream, heavily fished, but productive. Also fish offshore from bank or boat. Good accommodations and facilities.
Sioux	Wisconsin	U.S. 2 State 13	Ashland	June-Sept. Best bet to stay at Ashland where accommodations and facilities good; both limited at Washburn and Bayfield, but fish offshore between these points as well as in river.
Split Rock	Minnesota	U.S. 61	Two Harbors	May-Sept. Limited accommodations and facilities at Two Harbors, very limited at Beaver Bay. Fish offshore around lighthouse.

Sucker	Minnesota	U.S. 61	Duluth Two Harbors	May-Sept. Good accommodations and faciliites at Duluth, limited at Two Harbors. Fish lower river, offshore at mouth.
Tawas	Michigan	U.S. 23	Tawas City	April-June; Nov.-Dec. Also fish Tawas Bay from bank or boat. Good accommodations and facilities.
Two Hearted	Michigan	State 123	Newberry	May-Sept.; Nov. Limited accommodations and facilities at Newberry, very limited closer to stream at Deer Park and Two Heart, on county road 37, which gives access to river. An extremely productive and reliable steelhead stream, well worth the trip.
White	Michigan	U.S. 31	Whitehall Montague	April-June; Nov. Limited accommodations and facilities at mouth, very limited in upper reaches accessible via county road 86. Be sure to fish lake at mouth and offshore.

Now, to repeat an earlier suggestion, if you are planning to go into an area new to you, be sure to make inquiries locally as to current conditions. While seasons stay fairly constant, one area or another may suddenly have a tremendous run of fish and anxious steelheaders will flock there in a manner never before experienced. Inquiry by mail or phone takes a little time or effort, and often saves a great deal of frustration.

4

Starting Out for Steelhead

Veterans of the steelhead rivers won't need this chapter; they might find something new in it, but it's principally aimed at the novice. Those familiar with the rivers and the climate of the areas where steelhead fishing is best will know how important it is to go prepared. Those accustomed to warmer streams and less obstreperous weather are sometimes hard to convince that equipment and precautions which elsewhere would be merely a nuisance are necessary for the comfort and sometimes the safety of anglers fishing steelhead country.

There's no real need for much special gear or tackle if you're planning to join the growing number of summer steelhead enthusiasts. All you really need is the kind of tackle you'd normally use for bass fishing, plus a pair of felt-soled waders and an extra jacket. More detailed remarks about tackle will be found in the later chapters devoted to the several styles of steelheading. But, if you're going after winter steelhead, that's another story.

Winter steelhead fishing and comfort are mutually exclusive. They can't coexist. The best steelhead fishing is yours when trout and bass enthusiasts are contentedly lolling beside the fire, telling tall tales of last summer's adventures and indulging in dreams of next year. A summer fisherman doesn't realize that his tallest tale or wildest dream will pale beside the experiences that are waiting for him on a winter's day on a brawling river rushing to the ocean or a big lake under gray, unfriendly skies.

It's true that winter steelheading is available under conditions to make the most hardened duck-hunter shudder. It's fishing that visits on the unprepared the discomforts of frostbitten toes, chilblained fingers, windburned faces, and refrigerated joints. Under attack by the cold wind sweeping along the surface of the stream, the fisherman stands up to his midsection in greenish water whose icy chill seeps through his insulated waders, or crouches in a boat wondering why his quilted parka doesn't keep him warm. His hands are red and raw from intimate contact with wet fishing line, his nose is numb and running, his kidneys aching, and his knees cracking against each other like waterlogged castanets.

All of these discomforts are forgotten when the steelhead strikes. There occurs then a physical and psychic reaction that defies rational explanation. Suddenly, he feels no pain. The line sings off the reel, the fish leaps, far downstream. Cold feet, raw hands, and running nose are forgotten as the fisherman wonders anxiously whether the steelhead will stop its run before getting into the very heavy broken water at the riffle's tail, where he can't possibly handle the fish.

Clinging to his bucking rod, the angler quickly studies his reel, calculating the amount of backing already stripped off, trying to decide whether his terminal tackle will take the strain and hoping that the other fisherman a hundred yards downstream, where the hooked steelhead is jumping by this time, will reel in fast enough to avoid a leader-snapping foul-up. The backing keeps melting off the reel as the steelhead reaches the first heavier currents. The fisherman must decide at once whether to try to handle his fish from where he's standing, or follow it downstream, slipping on mossy rocks, perhaps falling down when he steps into a pothole and getting his boots or waders full of icy water.

Whatever he decides to do, there's no room in his mind for any problem not directly connected with the six or eight pounds of unhappy steelhead plunging on the line and threatening to return without a by-your-leave to the ocean he's so recently left. This is no fish reared in fresh water, but a battler just in from a year or two of training in the world's toughest school of survival, the ocean. It's an old salt with muscles toned fine from pursuing food and instincts sharpened from being pursued by bigger fish that want to eat it. An ocean-conditioned steelhead brings to its fight against rod and line a vigor and endurance that no freshwater fish can match. And in that fight it's aided by its habitat, for its instinct leads it to use the river's heaviest currents by heading into them and forcing the angler to fight water as well as fish.

For a moment the reel stops singing as the steelhead holds bottom in a stretch of quiet water. The fisherman breathes again, and starts backing toward shore, hoping to gain a position that will give him more freedom to move. Before the soles of his waders touch dry land the reel handle begins spinning wildly once more, catching a knuckle as the fish takes off again, but the man holding the rod doesn't even feel the scrape; he's too concerned about that lost line to let the loss of a few shreds of skin bother him. The skin will grow back, but if too much line is lost, that steelhead will be gone forever.

He gets to the banks and runs downstream, reeling as he goes, pausing when the fish pauses, regaining a few precious yards of line with every step and every stop. Splashing through shallow ponds along the bank, he showers himself thoroughly. His shirt is wet, and he can feel cold water trickling down his butt inside his waders; his face is redder than ever, his hands burn and his fingers are battered from the revolving reel handle, but inside he's warm. His blood is racing, heart pumping, eyes glowing. All of his attention is concentrated on the nine feet of arced rod he grasps in those numbed hands, on the singing reel, and the fish at the end of his taut line.

After twenty to forty minutes comes the payoff. Whether it's frustrating or rewarding depends on the size of the steelhead, the speed of the current, the skill of the fisherman, and the breaking-point of his terminal tackle. If he hasn't lost the fish, the angler has brought it slowly upstream and toward the bank, giving and regaining line in alternate spine-tingling spurts, lowering his rod when the steelhead clears water in a burst of spray. Now, there's only fifteen or twenty feet between the fish and the rod-tip. As the fish has tired, the fisherman has been working his way toward a level stretch of bank; if he hooked the fish while in a boat, he's wisely beached the craft and stepped on shore to finish the battle.

Finally the moment comes when the steelhead, exhausted, begins to turn on its side. This is the moment of danger, for the fisherman is tired, too, anxious to bring the fight to its conclusion. Even now, the steelhead has enough energy left to make a final try for freedom. When it feels the bottom gravel scraping its belly, it gives one final lunge, heading for the safety of deep water. Unless the angler is prepared, ready to yield line again, the odds momentarily favor the fish.

But the last desperation run is usually short; all the angler needs to do in most cases is to lower his rod tip, keeping a careful thumb on his reel in case the fish has more strength than most do at this point. When the final run has been checked, and his rod vertical again, the angler makes a quick backward run and gives a heave, sliding the fish out of the river and across the cold gravel of the bank. Quickly he drops his rod, picks up the beached fish, gives it a spine-cracking tap with a big rock at the base of its head, and holds up his trophy to admire.

Now, the purpose of this chapter is to put you in the waders of that successful fisherman. Not in terms of tackle and technique, these will come later when we explore the gear and methods used in different styles of fishing, but in terms of your personal relations with the environment in which you'll be operating. If you're not prepared when you hit a steelhead stream, you're going to be so miserable that you'll worry more about your physical discomfort than you will about catching fish. And, if you don't know what to look for when you set out to read steelhead waters, you might as well stay home. Most of the personal items you'll need will probably already be in your closet, if you indulge in any sports activity that takes you out in all kinds of weather. Reading a steelhead stream isn't as difficult as you might think, once you've learned to set aside what you've come to think of as productive water when seeking trout or bass.

Residents of steelhead country will tell you quite sincerely that theirs is the most equable climate in the world, ranging from average high temperatures of 68 degrees in summer to average lows of 36 degrees in winter. By the thermometer, they're right, but the thermometer they read isn't on the surface of a steelhead river. Whether the river flows into the Pacific Ocean or Lake Michigan or Lake Superior, the world's most cutting winds sweep up its surface, penetrating the average cold-weather clothing as though it was sewn from a few layers of cheesecloth.

On many mornings when the thermometer registers what anyplace else would be a moderately cool 40 to 45 degrees, you will crunch hard ice underfoot as you walk across the graveled bank of a stream toward the water. When you start fishing, your wet line will freeze to the guides; never mind what the thermometer says, meterologists have belatedly discovered what they call the "chill factor." This factor, computed by a combination of surface and wind temperatures, wind velocity and cloud cover, states the temperature in terms of its effect on human bodies. On an average winter day in steelhead country, a temperature of 45 degrees results in a chill factor that may be as low as 5 or 10 degrees.

Even summer steelheaders should observe the precaution of wearing a good wool shirt, long-johns, and carrying a windbreaker jacket. A thermometer reading of 68° a mile from the river is often converted to a chill factor of 35° on the surface of the stream. Summer or winter, being dressed in a way that insures your comfort allows you to give all your attention to fishing, and that's a sizable percentage in your favor when steelheading.

There's another important item you should keep in mind, even more important than comfort, and that's your personal safety. Precautions that would be foolishly elaborate on small, tame rivers and on lakes must become routine for the steelhead angler. Most fishermen at some time or other make mistakes on the water while wading or fishing from a boat, and grin sheepishly later on when telling about them. The man who makes mistakes on a big steelhead river won't be around later to admit his errors. These streams claim lives every season, and most of those lives are lost unnecessarily, simply through lack of understanding and lack of respect for the frightening power concealed in the fast currents and rocky bottoms of these rivers.

This isn't Nervous Nellie talk. I've lost good friends in steelhead rivers, men who should have known better, but who got over-confident and careless. There is nothing more tragic than preventable loss of life, and 99.99 percent of all accidents on steelhead streams need never happen.

Let's start out with wading. More steelheaders fish in boots or waders than from boats, and it's very difficult to stay high and dry when you're chasing a running fish downstream. You cannot select your footing with deliberation as you splash through pools and pot-holes under a full head of steam; there's always the danger that you'll try to run in the shallows instead of taking those extra two or three steps backward that will put you high and dry on the bank. Some-where along the way downstream, there's a good probability that you'll encounter a backwashed pool cut by an eddy or strong cur-rent, and that pool could be deeper than you are tall. You take a chance, step into it, and before you can step back the current has you.

When you run along the bank following a fish, don't go out even a few feet into the stream. If you must cut a few yards from the river to avoid a finger of water, keep in mind that it might not be a finger, but an arm. Give more line, hold your rod high, and skirt the pool rather than trying to cut through it.

When wading a river in steelhead territory, have a lot of respect for its power. Bottom conditions and swift currents on almost all these streams demand that you make haste slowly. In very few of them is the water completely clear; usually by the time you're knee-deep, you can't see your feet. If you can't see your feet, you can't see the riverbed, which in Pacific coastal streams will be lined with algae-slick rocks, and in Great Lakes streams studded with sunken logs.

Either footing is treacherous, and a misstep or even a foot planted without testing the surface it must rest on will send you sliding down to the bottom. Many veterans of steelhead rivers refuse to wear anything higher than hip boots as a precaution against letting their enthusiasm persuade them to go too far out. Some of them have learned through frightening experience that strength, agility, skill, and experience combined won't match the current's powerful pull.

If you're confident that you have enough self-control to avoid this trap, chest waders should be your choice. Insulated waders are a wise investment; the water runs cold in steelhead streams, and after a prolonged stay in it even insulated waders don't cut the chill. The best substitute for insulated waders is three pairs of socks. Put on first a pair of thin woolen socks, next a pair of silk or nylon, and top the sandwich with a pair of thick woolen ones. Even in stocking-foot waders, this combination will keep your feet reasonably warm. There are special wading socks made from foam plastic, but not everybody can wear them. If your feet sweat, you'll find these foam jobs getting pretty cold and clammy after you've worn them for an hour or so.

Over your socks, pull on two pair of woolen long-johns. Thermal underwear seems to lose its efficiency when worn inside waders, but wool still works. Slip into a pair of denim or covert-cloth jeans, and your legs will stay comfortably warm. Above the waist, your best bet is to put on clothing in layers. A wool undershirt, a thin wool shirt next to it, and a thick wool shirt on top will do the job. On very windy days, wear a parka-type jacket with a rainproofed outer shell over the second shirt.

When the weather's really cold and the wind unusually biting, which is about half the time, you can slip a small handwarmer into each breast pocket and each hip pocket. These are worth their weight in gold when you're bank-fishing or in a boat and can't depend on motion to keep your blood from congealing. If this sounds like an exaggerated list of clothing, it isn't. I've been warmer on deer stands in a deep snow at 8000-foot altitudes with the thermometer at ten degrees wearing a lot less clothing than I've found necessary on a steelhead river with the temperature at 45 degrees. And I'm not cold-sensitive by nature.

Now that you're dressed for it, let's wade. First, if the stream you're fishing is on the Pacific Coast, you must have felt soles on those waders or boots you're wearing. Categorically and emphatically, do not under any circumstances step into a western steelhead river wearing rubber-soled footwear. On many Great Lakes streams, rubber soles are satisfactory, but felts are so much safer in any stream that you're far better off using them 100 percent of the time. Felt soles give safe footing on any kind of bottom, and are the least costly insurance you can buy. Hobnail wading shoes, now just about out of fashion, are a little better than rubber soles, but you're safest in sticking to felt soles for any and all wading you do.

Felts can be applied to rubber-soled waders; there are do-it-yourself kits available for this purpose. The kits are very satisfactory; I used one to felt-sole a pair of rubber waders and the application endured nearly ten years of three to four times a week wear. There are also two or three kinds of strap-on felt-soled sandals that can be worn over regular wading boots.

Now, at the risk of being repetitive, once again: do not try to wade a steelhead stream unless you're wearing felt-soled footwear. This isn't just a personal opinion, but the consensus of 99.99 percent of all steelhead fishermen who wade. The other .01 percent wears hobnailed wading boots. Unfortunately, those who persisted in wearing rubber-soled boots aren't around any longer to register an opinion.

For all I've said by way of warning, there is a way to wade a steelhead river safely You don't step out boldly, but move sideways, like a crab, keeping your legs straight and always facing the current. You move with very short steps, lifting your feet only an inch or so off the bottom, and you constantly test your new footing before shifting your weight. You slide your foot along the streambed, feeling for loose small gravel that the current might wash out from beneath a freshly placed foot, and you probe with your toe for potholes and sudden drop-offs that are found with great frequency in these rivers. If your foot encounters a big moss-covered boulder, you scrape it with your boot-sole's edge before stepping on it, and you test it by lifting your weight experimentally to make sure the boulder won't tilt or roll.

Carrying a wading staff doesn't brand you as a timid soul on a steelhead stream. A limb cut from a handy tree will do in a pinch, but the best wading staff is one made from heavy-duty aluminum tubing that will bear your full weight without buckling. Your staff will have a weighted tip to help keep its point down, and a cork grip that will not only be kind to your hands, but will keep the staff afloat if you lose it and haven't had the foresight to attach it to your suspenders with a lanyard.

I belong to the group of fishermen who refuse to wade steelhead water without a staff. It's invaluable as a third leg, as a prop on which you can lean to rest your legs—one at a time—after a long period of standing in heavy current while casting. It's also a necessary tool with which you can feel ahead and probe out the nature of the river's bottom. With felt soles, a wading staff, and a lot of respect for the river to keep you from taking any chances, you can wade safely.

Now, about that boat you own and want to take on your trip to steelhead country. After all, you bought it for fishing, so why not use it? Fine—if you're a very good boatman. There are places where a boat is handy, others where it's really necessary. This is true of all steelhead waters, no matter where you might be fishing.

In Great Lakes and Pacific Coast rivers alike, the lower stretches of many very productive streams can often be fished only from a boat. A lot of good steelhead rivers flatten out near their mouths into slower, deeper water than is encountered upstream and the key spots can be reached only from a boat. A large number of Great Lakes steelhead rivers terminate in lakes or lagoons, as do some western rivers, and the fish hanging in these broad waters can be taken by trolling, or perhaps by casting or still-fishing. A reasonably competent boatman can handle a craft in these rivermouth areas without asking for trouble, and will have the satisfaction of being able to get out to where the steelhead are lurking.

Think twice or even three times, though, before setting out to pilot your own boat upstream, no matter how highly you regard your boatmanship. While you're thinking, ask yourself a couple of questions. Are you skilled in reading the surface signs of a river you've never seen before? Can you interpret the bulge in the water that warns you of a submerged shelf or rock waiting to rip out your bottom or at best shear off a prop-pin? Have you had a lot of experience taking a craft through rough, white water, upstream and down?

If your answers are honest and affirmative, and you figure the risk worthwhile, then set out in your boat—but wait until a local boatman starts upstream and follow him closely, letting him show you the channel. If your answers are honest but dubious, hire a local boat operator. The chances are you'll find he's also a guide, and while he's got his own boats, he'll go along with your wish to fish from your own familiar craft. If your answers are honest and negative, then hire a boatman-guide on the stream where you plan to fish. You'll have a better trip, a safer trip, in a boat that was built for the kind of water on which you'll be going. You'll also catch more fish.

One of the big jobs a guide will do for you is to teach you how to read a steelhead river. No matter how vast your experience in trout or bass waters, you have both learning and unlearning to do when you get to steelhead country. A steelhead river is not a trout stream and while the steelhead belongs to the trout family, it has habits and characteristics common to no other member of the clan. Most trout and bass are taken from pools where the fish lie resting, or from the tailwater or riffles where white water becomes calm, and morsels of food that have bounced in the upstream currents slow down for the waiting fish. Both trout and bass make their homes in the water from which you will take them; as has been noted earlier, the steelhead is only using the river as a suburbanite uses a commuter train or freeway.

Since they are constantly on the move, steelhead are not as spooky as most game fish. Footsteps on the riverbanks, loud noises, shifting of feet in a boat, do not put them down, nor do sloppy, splashing, water-ticking casts. Moving upstream, the fish travel in schools, or runs, which may string out for a mile of river or may be concentrated into a few hundred yards. The runs may be spaced closely, or far apart; there are no rules that will help you figure this out, except that when you stop getting strikes on what has been a hot riffle, it's time to move upstream.

It requires no mathematical ability, given the average speed of movement contained in an earlier chapter, to figure out how far upstream to move so that you'll be waiting when the fish arrive. Unlike trout, steelhead do not hang in protected water for long periods. They do stop to rest in riffles having large boulders that break the current, but seem to favor no one riffle over another in a given stream as their rest-stops.

In their upstream movement, as in so many matters piscatorial, the fish do not always go strictly by the book, but the movement of steelhead runs is generally a predictable proposition. A run may move two miles or four or six in the course of a 24-hour period, and it usually takes only a little bit of scouting to keep abreast of a good run, once you've located it.

Locating the fish that first time—reading the water, if you prefer to use the experts' cliché—involves several factors. Overall, your first job is deciding whether or not a given stream is even fishable, and this is a matter of color. Because rains are frequent in steelhead territory, rivers often get muddy and roiled in a matter of hours. They become brown with silt; the fish lurk stubbornly, inactive, uninterested. When rivers are brown, even veteran steelheaders stay home. As the stream clears it passes through several color stages. The brown fades to a light yellow, at which point bait fishing becomes possible. Then the yellow gives way to a milky, whitish-green cast; at this stage, bait fishing improves and lures have a good chance. Finally, the milky cast vanishes, the river takes on a green or green-blue hue, and becomes as clear as any steelhead stream ever gets in the wintertime. It is now that the fly fisherman can join the other anglers.

In choosing a spot to fish, it's again necessary to forget lessons learned while seeking trout or bass. Shun the calm pools and concentrate on the riffles, both those that flow over shallowly submerged rocks and those where touches of white water show. In addition to the riffles, look for long, deep glides where the current moves fast; these are usually to be found at places where the banks curve sharply, and where major rock formations or sandbars or gravelbars jut out into the stream. As you learn to read the water, you will be able to spot these bars even when they are submerged. The water is shallow over many of them, and more often than not the bar will be joined to the bank by a spit along which you can wade out, reaching the main bar, thus being able to cast to the glide.

Many of these bars occur in tidewater areas of steelhead rivers, and before you wade out, be sure to check the tide tables. On more than one occasion, I've gotten so engrossed in fishing that I waited too long past the tidal turn, and have been trapped on a bar when the incoming tide covered the spit I followed out with water too deep to wade. Two or three times, I've been rescued by passing boats; other times, I've gritted my teeth, held the contents of my pockets high, and waded to shore in water-filled waders.

One more point to keep in mind when looking for a place to fish is that trout-stream protocol, which requires you to leave a pool in possession of the angler who got there first, doesn't apply on steelhead rivers. On trout water, where only a few spots such as head and tailwaters and eddies might be productive, the custom makes sense. It doesn't make sense when an entire riffle or glide almost certainly holds fish for its entire length.

Fish where you see other fishermen; they'll make room for you, and you can tell by their spacing the polite amount of elbowroom to leave between you and your nearest neighbor. You'll also learn, by watching those who arrived first, what lures or flies happen to be producing. Of course, when someone up or downstream gets a strike, you'll join your neighbors as they reel in; it takes a lot of room to play a steelhead.

Always keep in mind the fish's habits. It's not hanging in the water waiting for food, but traveling. Fast water slows it down, and at least gives it time to look at your offerings; through calm stretches, it's jet-propelled. Nor do you work your lure experimentally, at various depths, to find the fish. The only depth worth working when steelheading is the bottom. Your bait or lure must be down there with the fish, otherwise you're not really fishing. You're just going through the motions.

Steelhead, eating while on the move, are very much like people who eat on the run; they take their food in snacks, rather than complete meals. Stomach studies referred to earlier show caddis larvae to be the food they most often consume, these larvae being found in the stomachs of almost 90 percent of the fish examined. Salmon roe, the bait fisherman's standby, was in about 60 percent of the stomachs. Beetles and flying insects made up the remainder of the stomach contents in the fish inspected. In none of them were there minnows or fry.

Streamside dissection of landed fish, so helpful in determining what to offer trout or bass, doesn't help the steelheader much. It's known that the fish eats very little, and that what it does eat comes from the insect-poor streams exclusively. The stomach studies do show that minnows aren't a factor in the steelhead's diet, which inspires the lure fisherman to avoid the bass-plug type lures that are copies in more or less detail of actual minnows. Yet, fishermen take steelhead regularly on spinners and wabblers that everyone agrees imitate the flashing movement of small fish; the shine of metal seems to have a fatal attraction for steelhead.

However definitive otherwise, the stomach studies offer no answer to the perennially debated question of why fish that don't eat minnows hit this type of lure. We're left where we were, with one school of thought claiming the fish hit lures out of anger, another attributing the strike to curiosity, and a third theorizing that the steelhead must eat smaller fish while in the ocean. Your guess is as good on this subject as that of the steelheading veteran or the fisheries biologist.

One thing the stomach studies prove conclusively is that knowledge of the steelhead's eating habits doesn't help you much in catching them. Experience bears this out, for I've gone through days when the steelhead, like all other fish, would spurn everything offered, and other days when they would hit anything striking the water. I recall a day on the Rogue where on the riffle I was fishing, seven of us had steelhead on at the same time; later, comparing notes, we found that each of us was using a different type of lure.

At another time, on Michigan's Big Manistee River, I was taking pictures while Ralph Fairbanks and Lud Frankenberger did the fishing. The Big Manistee is studded with sunken log-snags from the area's early lumbering days; it can be fished best from a boat anchored upstream from productive water, using a buoyant-bodied lure that will be carried deep downstream by the current, riding over snags or meeting them so gently that a twitch of the line will free the lure. Ralph and Lud both knew the stream well, and both were using the same style of presentation, alternating lures between a Flatfish and a Tadpolly; when both had the same lure in the water they usually used different colors. In spite of the fact that there was seldom more than one lure of the same type or color in the water at the same time, when we tallied strikes at the end of the day there was a difference of only one in the number of hits each had received.

It just may be, at this point, that you've decided no fish is worth learning all one needs to know and taking all the precautions recommended for steelhead fishing. Well, the dissertation on the steelhead's habits has been designed to help you think like a fish, the warnings and precautions to help you land your fish, after you've found it, in comfort and safety. But it is true that winter steelheading requires its followers to break rules they've learned while catching other fish, and to operate under conditions uncommon to angling.

Before you decide that these conditions are going to keep you from giving steelheading a try, answer a few more questions honestly. Did you ever tie into a trout that ripped off a hundred yards of line in his first run after feeling the hook? Did you ever encounter a bass that gave you eight tail-dancing leaps and snapped a ten-pound leader the last time it cleared water? Did you ever hook a muskie or pike weighing less than ten pounds that required a half hour of skillful playing before you landed it?

These are experiences you get only from steelhead. No matter how much trouble you go to in dressing, equipping yourself, taking special care on the stream; no matter how cold the weather or how raw the hands, the steelhead is worth every bit of the effort you must put forth to take it.

After you've hooked and landed a few, you'll agree.

5

The Steelhead and Bait

There was a time, and the time was no so long ago, when all steel-head fishing was done with bait. Before the advent of the spinning reel and reliable monofilament line, there were few fishermen endowed with the patience to master a bait-casting reel in the way it had to be used, with the heavy water-absorbing lines that were the only ones then available, in order to fish lures in the big steelhead rivers. It was a clumsy combination of tackle at best, and relatively few became experts with it. For many years, steelheading meant plunking in a blob of bait and settling back to wait until a fish noticed it.

Because almost all steelheaders fished with bait, the legend and belief were born that the most fish and the biggest fish were taken by the man with bait on his hook. This is no more true of steelhead fishing than it is of fishing for trout or bass with worms and minnows. Bait fishing was no more of a guarantee of success then than it is now, despite the insistence of today's grizzled old-timers that the best—and some of them claim the only—way to take the steelhead is with salmon roe. There is actually less bait fishing done of steelhead streams today than there was ten or fifteen years ago, and plenty of fish are still being taken.

These dedicated bait fishermen are usually men who grew up in steelhead country, who have spent long years in mastering the bait-fishing techniques, and they hold to their beliefs as firmly as does the trout fishing purist who insists that the only proper way to take a trout is on a dry fly. As practiced by them, the use of bait is an art; in many ways, the use of bait in steelhead fishing requires a nicer touch, far more experience, and a great deal more practice than do lure or fly fishing. And taken in the context of stream conditions of the area, bait fishing for steelhead is as valid and sportsmanlike as any other method, always with the stipulation that the tackle used be suited to the waters and the fish.

During the winter steelhead season rains are very common. It also rains during the summer steelhead season, but not with the frequency and intensity that is characteristic of the winter months. This results in the rivers being roiled for a very high percentage of the time, and there will be days—perhaps weeks—when the fish's circle of vision is eight to twelve inches in diameter. The chances of the steelhead seeing a fly in roiled water are virtually nonexistent, and of seeing even a brightly flashing lure only slightly better. Fly fishermen can count on being able to peddle their fur-and-feather confections on perhaps 25 percent of the days in a six-month season; lure fishermen have a sporting chance on 50 percent of the days; but the bait fisherman is in business 80 percent of the time.

When it thus becomes a question of fishing with bait part of the time or not fishing at all, the most devoted purist or dedicated lure fisherman follows the sage advice to relax when facing the inevitable. They may enjoy it less, but they'll shrug and head for the bait box.

Although few anglers are cost-conscious where their sport is concerned, it might also be well to remark that bait fishing requires much less expenditure than lure fishing. It also requires less effort than the fly fisherman puts into making the long casts needed to cover a big river. Nor are all bait fishermen frustrated fly and lure men; plenty of them fish bait because they're convinced it's more productive, or just because they like to. On any steelhead stream you care to name, the bait fisherman will find a lot of others using roe. He'll find bait fishing productive, if he is willing to learn how to present his bait properly, and spinning tackle has taken away most of the effort that was involved in presentation.

There are two styles of bait fishing common to steelheading. One is variously called "mooching" or "drifting," and the other is known as "plunking." Both names are as descriptive as could be hoped for.

Mooching is the art of allowing a roe cluster or a single salmon egg to drift along the bottom of a stream, manipulating rod and line to keep the bait bumping along a few inches above the rocks and just a trifle slower than it would normally be carried by the current. Mooching was done originally from boats drifting downstream. Today, the more sophisticated tackle available than when this style of fishing originated makes it easy to mooch from the banks. Both names used to describe this style of bait presentation are used interchangeably and loosely in connection with either bank or boat fishing.

Plunking is fishing with a stationary, or anchored, bait. The roe-decorated hook is held in place in a likely riffle or glide by a sinker just heavy enough to keep the bait on the bottom, yet not heavy enough to interfere with the angler's recognition of the gentle tugs of a taking fish. Of the two types of bait fishing, plunking is the more difficult to master, since the steelhead approaches a stationary bait in a slow and stealthy fashion.

Like all steelheading, bait fishing produces cold hands and wind-reddened faces, watering eyes, and a running nose. It also produces a lot of good fish. Both styles of bait fishing require concentration and persistence, and in learning both styles the angler must be prepared to invest a certain amount of his time in preliminary practice. It takes a certain amount of experience, when drifting roe, to cover the water thoroughly by spacing casts and manipulating the rod and reel. When plunking, it takes time and experience to acquire the delicate sensitivity of feel that allow a fisherman to tell the difference between the tugs of changing currents and those of a taking fish; current and underwater debris brushing the line often feel more like a steelhead at the bait than does the fish itself.

Methods used in mooching and plunking have changed very little since fishermen first began taking steelhead on bait; the changes that have taken place are those dictated by improved tackle. Zane Grey, writing about his 1918 experiences on a Washington steelhead stream, describes the kind of tackle used before the spinning reel became commonplace. It consisted of a heavy fly rod with a multiplying bait-casting reel attached, the reel filled with enameled silk fly line. Casting from the reel with such a rig is obviously difficult; the fisherman wore a basket strapped to his waist, and stripped line loosely into the basket so that the drag of the line through the small guides of the fly rod would not shorten his cast. Of course, the relatively stiff fly line would often tangle itself up in the basket, but this rig did make possible the long casts necessary. Today, a comparative novice with a spinning rod and reel can outdistance the casts possible with the prespinning rigs.

Before getting into the subject of tackle, let's dispose of the bait question. Topping the list of the steelhead's preference is salmon or steelhead roe in clusters, followed by single salmon eggs, and in tidewater or in lagoons single small shrimp or a tiny anchovy fillet. Worms are seldom effective; worms do not have for steelhead the magnetic attraction they do for freshwater trout. Occasionally, a summer-run steelhead will take a worm, especially when the presentation is by drifting. Minnows are uncommon as steelhead bait, even in the mouths of rivers and lagoons.

Roe fishing is no longer confined exclusively to steelhead streams, though when it was I often encountered anglers who had never heard of roe bait and did not know where roe comes from. This tremendously popular, odorous, gluey, and effective steelhead bait is, of course, the eggs of the female salmon. Efforts have been made to popularize salmon roe as a substitute for caviar, but on its taste in this connection I'm unable to comment; after having used it as steelhead bait for so many years the memory of the smell it leaves on an angler's hands has inhibited me from trying it.

Salmon and steelhead roe are both used for bait, and veteran bait fisherman really prefer the latter. There being no commercial fishery, the supply of steelhead roe depends on the catches of individual anglers, who either process the roe cases themselves or pass them along to bait-fishing friends. Salmon roe is, of course, one of the by-products of commercial fishing, eggs from the ripe females being saved when the fish are cleaned. Salmon eggs are processed as whole roes or as individual eggs; steelhead eggs are too small to be used singly, and only the whole roe cases are processed.

Preservation of the roes is very simple. When whole sacs are being prepared, they are allowed to air-dry for a few hours after being taken from the fish, then sprinkled with alum to toughen the sac's membranous outer covering. Fresh-frozen roe is the preferred bait, and it is put into containers for freezing as soon as the egg sacs can be handled readily. If the roes are to be packaged in plastic packets or in jars, they are immersed in a warm brine solution; usually coloring is added which turns them from their normal light pink into a bright red. They are then sealed into their containers with a small quantity of fish oil added to the brine.

Home preservation of fresh steelhead roe is very simple. The egg sacs are air-dried for about two hours on a plate, platter, or enameled tray. They are turned once so all sides will dry. The roes are then sprinkled lightly on all surfaces with powdered alum and placed in a cool spot to cure for 24 hours. Home-preserved steelhead roe must be stored under refrigeration if not used at once. In the refrigerator, it will keep for two to three months.

Single-egg processing of salmon eggs is done in much the same manner used in preparing whole egg sacs. Only one preliminary step is involved, washing the eggs from the sacs under a very gentle stream of water to separate them from the jellylike mucous surrounding them. The eggs are then sprinkled with alum to toughen their outer membrane cover, and passed through a brine bath before being graded and sorted by size to be put into jars. Normally, salmon eggs range in color from a yellowish pink to a dark blushing pink. They are often dyed shades toning from orange to deep red, and sometimes fluorescent material is added to the dye.

Bait fishermen using single salmon eggs give first preference to the natural-colored ones, and choose the biggest sizes, those about ¼ inch in diameter. Single eggs have an "eye," a globule of oil, trapped inside the egg case; it is this oil escaping that lays down a scent trail when the eggs are in the water, and the eye should always be pierced by the hook when baiting up.

All roe, whether single eggs or clusters, will change color after being immersed in water. It is the extent of this change as well as its character that determines the quality of the roe used. The best roe will take on a milky pinkish hue after a short period in the stream, regardless of its original shade when taken from jar or package. It will exude a tiny stream of this "milk" into the water; this is comparable to the oil that escapes from the "eye" of single eggs, the scent trail which a steelhead passing downstream will hopefully follow to your hook. All roe baits should be changed often, for the scent trail fades after they have been in the water for a while.

Shrimp and anchovy baits, generally used only in tidewater or in lagoons, are usually trimmed to the smallest practical size compatible with the hook you are using. Shrimp, unless very small, should be split lengthwise into halves. Anchovies should be filleted and the fillets cut into strips no wider then ½ inch, and long enough to be threaded onto your hook and up its shank to the eye.

All the bait in the world isn't going to help you, though, if it isn't fished correctly. The right kind of tackle will help you make the most effective presentation. Happily, it's no longer necessary to use the clumsy gear described by Zane Grey as being typical of the 1918 period, though old-timers on steelhead streams remember having used the line basket in order to get out a suitably long cast. This kind of tackle vanished, along with the heavy surf rods and deep-sea reels filled with linen cuttyhunk line, when modern heavy-duty spinning rods and reels entered the angling picture. Today, even the veterans have decided they'd rather switch to modern tackle than fight the old-style gear.

Light spinning rods with sensitive and responsive tips yet still rugged enough to stand up to the strain of handling big fish in heavy water; reels with ball bearings and spool arbors of steel rather than babbit-metal; monofilament lines that minimize guide friction, current drag and water absorption; all contribute to the greater ease and pleasure enjoyed by the bait fisherman. Whether you intend to mooch or plunk, your choice of equipment will be very much the same; the tackle requirements for bait fishing by either method vary so slightly as to make no practical difference when you set out to acquire the items needed.

Look for what most manufacturers designate as a light surf rod or light boat rod, nine to eleven feet long. Pacific Northwest rivers make necessary the kind of long casts usually associated with ocean fishing, and have currents heavier than you're likely to encounter in even the most vicious offshore undertows. A nine-foot rod is about the minimum length you should consider. Not only does the length make long casts easier, it gives you more mobility at streamside. Steelhead fishing, especially in winter, is done when the rivers are at their highest, and the water is usually so far above its normal level that you will be working amid bushes that at low water are far from the banks.

It will often be necessary, even when you are wading, to manipulate your rod tip over bushes that are within your fishing area; this can happen to you both in casting and in playing a hooked fish. There are times when the long rod will allow you to avoid getting snarled in streamside growth, and to this advantage add the fact that you get a more delicate "feel" from the long, very flexible rod than you do from a rod that is sturdy but short and insensitive. Just be sure the rod you choose has enough backbone to allow you to feel a light-taking fish in heavy water. If you are drift fishing from a boat, the long rod has its advantages, too; you can swing your rod tip in a full circle to follow a fighting fish rather than having to shift positions in the boat or to pass the rod from hand to hand in order to avoid getting fouled at bow or stern.

It's difficult to be specific in listing the makes and exact models of rods suitable for steelhead bait fishing. Tackle manufacturers are constantly changing and improving their products, and each change usually involves an advertised rod designation or model number being changed, too. What is today called Doe Co.'s Preferred Rod Model 123 may tomorrow be called the Doe Co.'s Super-perfect Rod Model 456. Almost all of the firms manufacturing glass rods turn out satisfactory light surf and light boat rods suitable for steelhead bait fishing. Browning, Conlon, Fenwick, Garcia, Heddon, Shakespeare, South Bend, and others not listed make hollow glass laminate spinning rods of good quality. I've used the products of most of these and other manufacturers of nationally distributed rods and find little difference in their quality and performance.

Any of these makers' rods that fit the specifications already outlined will serve you well. You will find that most, if not all of them, have such desirable features as carboloy or tungsten butt and tip guides, locking reel seats, good slip-free cork grips, sturdy and well-fitted ferrules. The hollow fiberglass laminate rods sold today are of very uniform quality and almost uniform action. They are far removed from the soupy, flimsy, center-turned solid glass rods of a few years back, which gave all glass rods a bad reputation. You should, of course, avoid solid glass rods even if you're just going to fish for perch in a brook. You should also avoid the error made by many newcomers to steelhead country: the belief that spinning rods suitable for use with trout, bass, pike or muskie in small streams and lakes are suitable for use in steelheading. They aren't.

To wind up the rod question, for the benefit of those who still cling to the split bamboo rod, prospects for finding any suitable for use in steelhead bait fishing aren't encouraging. Most of the bamboo spinning rods today are built for light-tackle enthusiasts. There was at one time a vogue for fine bamboo bait-casting rods (not plug rods) and many makers turned out some beautiful jobs until about the middle 1920s. These were rods that ranged from seven to nine feet in length, some of them designed for bonefishing, others for minnow fishing in muskie waters, and they had the length and backbone that would make them suitable for steelhead bait fishing. Some of these rods are certainly still in existence, in dusty cases resting in attics or basements. If you should manage to come by one, use it and enjoy it.

To the best of my knowledge, the late E. C. "Pop" Powell was the first man to design and build bamboo rods for steelhead bait fishing. When I visited his shop in the early 1940s, he showed me a group of eight or ten heavy spinning rods varying in length from nine to eleven feet and having very fast, responsive tips. Somehow I never got around to ordering one of these rods, or even asking Pop what their history was and what became of them. However, such bamboo rod makers as Orvis, Winston, Payne, and Leonard and the few others still producing rods today could supply you, if you carry a bank in your hip pocket instead of the more usual wallet.

As important as the rod is the reel with which you equip it. Here there is no problem, for good heavy-duty spinning reels are available in great variety and quantity. Those designed for surf and sea fishing should be the only reels considered, since they will have the sturdiness to stand up under a steelhead's heavy plunges. They will also be corrosion-resistant, a key requirement, since you will quite probably be using them in brackish tidal waters. Most bait fishermen in steelhead country swear by the Garcia Mitchell Model 302 reel, which is designed for saltwater duty and is highly corrosion-resistant. The same manufacturer's Model 302 reel is almost as highly thought of; it is identical with the 306 in size and line capacity, but does not have anticorrosion construction.

Other manufacturers, including Berkley, Gladding, Mepps, Shakespeare, Heddon, and Wright & McGill, all make or import European reels of sturdiness and quality, which in their surf and sea fishing sizes have the line capacity called for in steelhead fishing. Your choice will depend on the reel you like best to use, feel at home with, or has been made by a favorite manufacturer. All that's important is that the handle shape suits you, that you find the drag arrangement convenient, and other minor matters, as long as the basic reel is sturdy and has large line capacity.

During recent years there has been a great boom in the closed-face spinning reel, and most manufacturers have brought out what they describe as "heavy-duty" or "saltwater" versions of this type of reel. I've stream-tested several makes, and have gotten the opinions of other anglers who have used not only the ones I've tried, but the products of different makers. Their opinions agree with my own: that in its present stage of development, the closed-face spinning reel is not for steelheaders. Most of them simply aren't rugged enough. Gears strip or bend, line jams on the spools, or the pickup mechanism goes sour. This type of reel is fine for trout or bass or other fish that don't perform with a steelhead's vivacity; I own a couple of closed-face reels and on lesser fish their performance is completely satisfactory. They just don't belong on steelhead rivers.

Many lure and bait steelheaders prefer a multiplying or bait-casting reel—in fisherman's vernacular, a "plug reel." Here the Garcia Ambassadeur 5000 and 6000 series reels are favored, along with the Heddon 499, which was designed with the steelhead fisherman's requirements in mind. Both the Garcia and Heddon reels have all the features, not the least of which is sturdiness, essential in any reel that will be used for steelhead.

There are so many good new monofilament lines on the market now that your choice boils down to a matter of individual preference. I've had consistently good results with Garcia's Platyl, with Stren and Trilene, and with several other less widely distributed brands. Your choice of line should be one of the high strength-to-diameter ratio monofils. You will want at least 200 yards of 20-pound test on your reel, and in any but the clearest water use it for leader as well as line. In clear water, it's sometimes necessary to go down to fifteen-pound monofil for leader. For use with plug reels, the most satisfactory braided line developed so far is Micron. It has an excellent test-to-diameter ratio, the 20-pound test being no bigger in diameter than the equivalent test in monofil. Micron lays out smoothly and straight, and will not pack or birdcage as monofilaments will when used on a bait-casting reel.

Getting at last to the business end of your tackle, the hooks you use are as important as everything else. The steelhead is one of the few fish you'll encounter that has the fighting strength to straighten a hook that is the least bit soupy or too softly tempered. A few years ago on the Deschutes in Oregon, I watched a nearby bait fisherman lose three fish in succession due to hooks that straightened out under pressure. After the third had made its getaway, I called over to ask the angler what kind of hook he was using, and he profanely replied that his hooks were a new kind that his regular tackle dealer had just gotten in. About this time, the fourth fish hit, was played a few minutes, and lost. When the unhappy fisherman reeled in, we both examined his hook; like the ones he'd used earlier, the bend had straightened just enough to allow the steelhead to pull free. I supplied him with a few good hooks, since all he had was the new kind he'd bought, and watched him hook and hold the next fish that struck.

One of the minor wonders of the fishing tackle business is that there are no American-made hooks which will compare with those turned out in England by Allcock and in Norway by Mustad. Both these firms offer a Model Perfect hook (the name is patented by Allcock, but the bend of the Mustad model is exactly the same) that is perfect for roe clusters; fishing this type of bait calls for a heavy hook to overcome the natural buoyancy of the cluster. The comparatively wide opening of the Model Perfect bend keeps the point of the hook free when you use this somewhat bulky bait, and the #2 wire from which the extra-stout hooks are forged is good insurance against any fish straightening them out.

Model Perfect hooks in sizes #2, #1, #1/0, and #2/0 stout should be in every bait fisherman's kit. So should a few Allcock Model Perfect light wire hooks, which are sometimes designated salmon dry fly hooks. These will hold as securely as the stout wire hooks; being springy rather than brittle they have no tendency to straighten. When fished with shrimp or anchovy fillets, the light wire hooks will keep the bait in better condition, since they do not tear it as the heavier versions do. When using these solid-flesh baits, some fishermen like to switch to a sproat bend hook, feeling that the smaller gap makes it easier to hide the hook inside the bait, but I've found no reason to change from Model Perfect in favor of the sproat bend.

A few diehards cling to the use of double or treble hooks for bait fishing, using sizes #2 and #1 in the doubles and #2, #3, or #4 in the trebles. After experimenting for several seasons with single, double, and treble hooks, I came to the conclusion that the single hook is best. I failed to hook a greater number of fish, or had more throw hooks during the fighting, when using doubles and trebles than was the case with singles. The percentage was not great, but it was definite. There's really no point in carrying a big assortment of hooks with you, when the Model Perfect in the sizes given will do very well for all baits except single salmon eggs.

For single eggs, you will want extra-stout wire egg hooks, and these are stocked by every tackle store in steelhead areas. Very similar to spider fly hooks, these short, sharply curved egg hooks can be almost completely buried in the big eggs most attractive to steelhead, and hold the eggs well. Extra-stout egg hooks in sizes #4 and #6 will be the only ones you'll need to carry; unlike the longer shanked hooks, which will have turned-down eyes, the egg hook eyes will be turned up. You will also have a choice of finishes in egg hooks: standard bronze, chromed, or gold-plated. After using all three finishes quite extensively, I haven't been able to discover that steelhead are at all choosy about hook color, if they like the looks of the egg impaled on it.

There are three important regional baits used in addition to the universally used roe bags and single salmon eggs. Two of these, shrimp and anchovy strips, seem confined to the Pacific Coast. The third, the Mayfly nymph, known in the region as a "wiggler," is a favorite of Great Lakes fishermen. The shrimp and anchovy baits are usually plunked downstream in wide, slow waters; they are also used in lagoons, threaded on a light wire 2x long #1 or #1/0 hook. A double or treble 2x long #1 or #1/0 hook is often used with anchovy strips. Wigglers are fished in the same style as single salmon eggs, on a short-shanked egg hook. Terminal tackle for shrimp and anchovy strips is rigged in the same manner as that for roe bags, and terminal tackle for the Mayfly nymph is rigged in the same fashion as that for single eggs.

There's one more piece of equipment seldom found in tackle stores outside steelhead country, but it's one that will save the tempers and ease the budgets of all steelhead bait fishermen. It's a simple little device, nothing more than a two-inch length of rubber surgical tubing attached to one of the eyes of a three-way swivel. The formal name of this fisherman's friend is the Klamath Cinch, but it's often referred to as a lead cinch or just a cinch. Tied between line and leader, the tubing of the cinch accepts the tip of a pencil sinker, and makes a rig that's virtually snagproof.

Cracks and rock crevices abound on the bottoms of steelhead rivers, just waiting to grab and hold any sinker that doesn't have perfectly straight sides. These clefts have a fatal attraction for cinch and bell sinkers; there must be tons of these rounded chunks of lead

A length of rubber surgical tubing is attached with fine wire to a T-swivel or three-way swivel to make the Klamath Cinch; in use, a pencil sinker is inserted in the open end of the tubing.

distributed over the bottoms of various steelhead streams. A pencil sinker in a cinch foils about 95 percent of these lead-traps; it will glide and slide over them without hanging up, thanks to the flexible rubber tubing holding it. Even when the sinker does get wedged between rocks, the tubing helps the angler snap it free; at worst, the sinker will be pulled from the tube as it stretches under pressure, but the terminal tackle is saved. The angler is spared the time and trouble of rigging a new hook and leader; he simply slips in another pencil sinker and goes on with his fishing. Sinkers cost less than hooks.

Any bottom fishing in fast-flowing streams that have rocky bottoms is going to result in a certain number of snag-ups, of course. Use of the cinch cuts this number to a minimum, and cuts almost to zero the number of times that hook and leader get lost along with the sinker. A substitute for the cinch can be made by attaching a pencil sinker to one eye of a three-way swivel with a short length of light monofil, but this arrangement will snap three times as often as will the cinch with its rubber tubing.

In drifting bait, the cinch is almost a necessity, for this type of presentation requires a fairly precise balance between sinker weight, water depth, and current speed. In shallow or slow-moving water, you might need only a small bit of sinker, weighing ¼ ounce; in faster and deeper riffles or glides up to two ounces might be required to keep your bait bumping properly along the bottom. Pencil sinkers come in weights up to three ounces; the longer the sinker, the heavier, and it's easy to get the proper weight by trimming this kind of sinker with a knife or pliers.

All this exhaustive exploration of the tackle best suited to steelheading isn't just idle indulgence; it has good reasons behind it. No other freshwater fishing demands the same careful attention to details; what would be niggling matters applied to other fish in other waters becomes important to your success on a steelhead stream. Time and again I've seen very good fishermen insist on using a favorite fly or spinning rod after being warned by guides or knowledgeable friends that these favorites were too light for steelhead fishing. While most of these men had proved their skill with their favorite gear by landing big bass or trout with it, they hadn't realized how tough a steelhead can be when hooked. Very few of these fishermen were able to repeat with a steelhead. Quite a number of them have not only lost hooked fish, but have had a prized rod or reel damaged.

Steelhead not only have the power to straighten soupy hooks; they are big enough and strong enough to snap rod tips, spring ferrules, and cause the gears of light-duty reels to jam under the strain they put on tackle. On a couple of occasions, I've seen reels with babbit-metal spool arbors freeze up after a succession of long, fast runs by hooked fish has worn the arbor unevenly. It takes only one such experience to make a believer out of the overconfident angler who tries to handle steelhead on tackle that's too light. If this long exposition convinces you that it's better to start out with the right kind of gear, if it helps you land fish that you might otherwise lose, or saves you from having a favorite rod broken, it will have served its purpose.

Not only must your rod and reel be sturdy enough to handle the strain put on them by big fish in big water, but your lines and leaders must be free from frayed spots and the knots you use must hold well without weakening your monofilament too greatly. If there's a weak link in your tackle anywhere between you and the steelhead, you can depend on the fish to take advantage of it.

After losing a number of good fish to bad knots, I finally narrowed down to three the number of knots I use. All are easy to tie with cold, wet hands; all have good holding qualities and resist slippage. These three knots also rank high in tests conducted by monofilament manufacturers to determine the effect various knots have in weakening line and leader material. The study included conducting breaking tests in all kinds and all diameters of monofilaments tied with the 20 most-used fisherman's knots.

A lot of highly regarded knots showed up pretty badly in these tests. The widely used turle knot, for instance, was shown to reduce

Figure 1

For line-to-line connection or line to leader-butt connection, use the perfection loop. To tie: form two loops in line or leader as shown in Figure 1; pull loop A through loop B as shown in figure 2 and pull firmly to tighten.

Figure 2

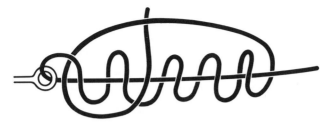

For leader-to-leader connections, use the blood knot. To tie: overlap leader ends about 2 to 3 inches, make three turns with each end around the standing length of leader, tuck ends through the gap between the two sets of turns, pull and work the turns and ends gently to tighten, trim ends flush with knot. Two cautions: make the turns in opposite directions for maximum strength, and do not pull leader fast when tightening or it may be weakened by friction.

For leader-to-hook connection, use the pendré, or modified jam knot. To tie: pass end of leader through eye of hook or lure, make six to eight turns around standing portion of leader; loop end back into gap between eye and first turn, then carry end through the gap between the standing leader (on which turns were made) and loop; pull and work the turns and ends gently to tighten, trim end flush with knot. When using this knot in lure-eyes and big hooks, many fishermen pass two turns through the eye. This makes the knot trickier to tighten, but gives extra holding power and insurance against fraying.

monofil strength by 27 percent when used to connect leader to hook. The double water knot, sometimes called the surgeon's knot, used to join line and leader, reduced breaking strength by 42 percent. Other popular knots cut the rated test of monofils by as much as 35 to 50 percent. You don't need to be a Nobel prize-winning mathematician to figure out what a 50 percent loss in strength means when you're fishing six-pound test leader.

Showing up best in the tests were three knots that will serve the angler for every purpose where a knot is needed. The blood knot, used to join two piece of monofil, such as tying line to leader or building tapered leaders for fly fishing, reduces the rated strength of the material by only thirteen percent. The perfection loop knot, used to make a quick change of dropper hooks and fly line to leader, cuts strength only twelve percent. And the pendre, or modified jam knot, for attaching hooks or swivels to monofilament, cuts the strength of the material by only two percent.

Of these three knots, only the pendre requires special attention in tying. It must be very carefully worked tight against the hook eye or swivel loop. All slack must be taken out of the loops while the knot is being clinched against the metal eye, and this must be done with a gentle, sustained pull. The loops formed, both the loop next to the metal and that made by bringing the running end of the knot back through the twists, must be tugged to keep them closed while the knot is being tightened. Even when these precautions are observed, the pendre is a quick and easy knot to tie. The other two knots are equally fast and simple to use, and when used in their proper places will let your monofilament retain the highest percentage of its rated test.

Rigging terminal tackle for drifting bait is simplicity itself. Attach a Klamath Cinch to the end of your line, an 18-inch length of leader to the second eyelet of its swivel, and your choice of a hook on the leader, using the pendre knot in all three places. Slip a pencil sinker into the tubing of the cinch, working the lead's tip into the tube

To rig terminal tackle for bait or lure fishing, attach one eye of the Klamath Cinch's swivel to the line or leader; on a 10-inch to 14-inch trace, attach baited hook or lure. Length of the trace is determined by water conditions, with the shorter length generally that required for bait fishing.

about ¼ inch. An equally effective method of rigging terminal tackle for bait-bouncing is to use an 18- to 24-inch length of 15-pound leader on your line, terminate the leader in one eye of a T-swivel or three-way swivel, attach your lead to the swivel-eye opposite the leader with a 10- or 12-inch length of 4- to 6-pound monofil and your hook to the third swivel-eye with 12 inches of 15-pound monofil. Your lead will drag bottom with either rigging, while your baited hook floats just above the streambed in the area where steelhead like to stay.

Bait-fishing with roe clusters or roe bags made at streamside was once a messy, smelly job that gave a lot of steelhead fishermen chilblained hands and chapped, cracked knuckles. Some made their bags at home, where they had soap and hot water with which to wash the smell off their hands, but for the most part the custom was to make the bags fresh, as they were used. Now, an automatic bait-bagger allows the angler to make roe bags anywhere without smearing his hands with roe. There are several versions of the roe-bagger available, all performing essentially the same function in slightly different ways. All of them are moderate in price, and pay for themselves many times over in removing the mess from what used to be a messy job.

Many old-time roe-fishermen swear there's no bait that works as well as freshly made bags. If you lack a bagger and are faced with the job of preparing roe baits, here's the procedure. Cut off a thumb-sized to walnut-sized chunk of roe, or use the equivalent in single salmon eggs. Put the roe in the middle of a three-inch square of red nylon mesh, pull up the corners and sides of the material, and tie them off with thread. This forms a bag about ¾ to one inch in diameter. The loose ends of the mesh are trimmed off above the tie. These ready-to-use balls of roe can be carried in a plastic bag in your tackle box—just make sure the bag doesn't leak.

At streamside, you can either make bagged roe baits or simply tie the roe to the hook with several fairly loose turns of thread. The bags can be formed right on the hook, tied just under its eye. When tying roe cluster baits to a hook without using mesh, be sure to include a strip of the egg sac membrane when you cut your cluster; this helps keep the bait together in the water.

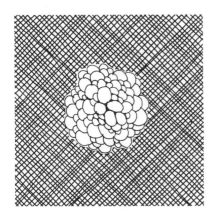 

Salmon roe in a square of nylon mesh is wrapped on the hook so that the points and barbs protrude from the bag; loose ends are trimmed off. This job can be done at home with a mechanical bagging device, or streamside.

Be sure, too, that you carry with you to the river a couple of big pieces of disposable rag or an old towel. Only a fisherman with an impaired sense of smell or a bad head cold will fail to wash his hands after baiting up. The odor that roe leaves on your hands is highly fishy and long lasting; I've found the best way to keep your hands in fairly good shape is to coat them with a thin layer of silicone-based dry fly dressing or line dressing. There are several hand-protectors sold at drug and cosmetic counters, the best known being Silicare and Lanolay, but even in their heavy-duty formulations these products are not as long-lasting as line dressing. If you overlook the precaution of coating your hands before handling roe, the best thing you can do is find a sandpocket at the water's edge and scour with it to remove the clinging smell.

Now, we're finally ready to drift that baited hook down a promising riffle or glide. You may need to make a short experimental drift or two in order to balance the weight of your terminal tackle properly. With your hook baited with clusters or a single egg, whichever you plan to use, see how your sinker behaves. If it sinks quickly and remains stationary, you're using too much weight. Trim the sinker and try again, until the lead sinks deliberately to the bottom and dances along it over the rocks. You can feel each bounce transmitted along your line through the tip of your rod. The bait should move at a speed slightly slower than the current, and always be in touch with the bottom.

All bait fishermen must remember that the steelhead is never more than a few inches above the streambed as it travels upstream. Nor is the fish primarily interested in eating; a meal or snack is just a sideshow to the main event of spawning. The trick is to put the bait right in the steelhead's face, where he can't help seeing it. This means fishing on the bottom and in live water, for while the steelhead does pause for brief rest periods in protected spots behind boulders and logs, it does not hang in these places waiting for food, as other game fish do. By preference, the steelhead is a live-water fish, not given to lurking long in backwashes and eddies.

If you're drifting from a boat, begin at the head of the riffle or glide. Drop your line in the water and let it run until you feel the sinker in contact with the bottom. Then let the current carry your boat through the productive area, the baited hook bouncing off the streambed behind you. Cover the entire riffle or glide in drifts a few yards apart, parallel to the bank. You must always feel the bottom of the river with your sinker; if your line slides swiftly and smoothly in the boat's wake, you're not deep enough to connect with a fish.

Drifting a bait from the bank is a matter of covering the productive water with a series of casts, beginning at the head of the riffle and working downstream to the tail. Begin with a long cross-stream cast, and let the weight of your terminal tackle carry a few extra yards of line with it as it settles to the surface. You can tighten your line, holding the rod almost vertically, after your lead finds bottom. The trick now is to keep in touch with that bottom as the current sweeps your line downstream and in a quarter circle back to the bank below the spot where you're standing.

(*On facing page*) This casting pattern will serve you for all bank fishing in streams, whether using bait, lures, or flies. You are standing at the point marked A. Your first cast should take bait, lure, or fly very near the opposite bank, and be allowed to work downstream to the point where the current's action starts to draw the lure back to your side of the river. Most of the strikes will come in the zone shown by the black bar, or just above it. On succeeding casts, shorten line to work the entire width of the stream.

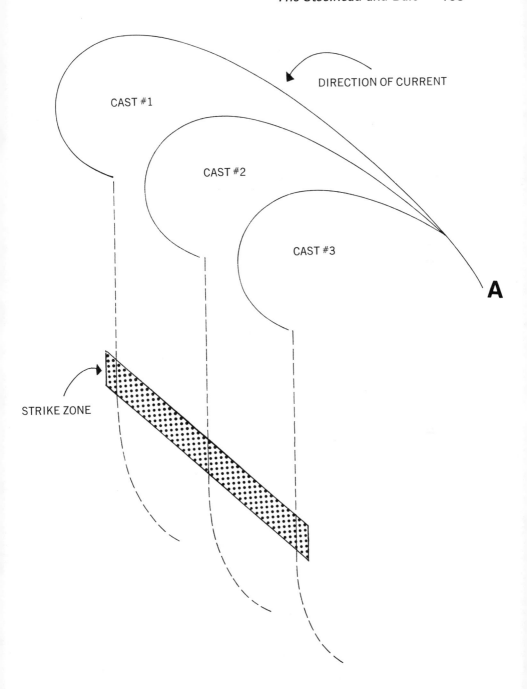

DIRECTION OF CURRENT

CAST #1

CAST #2

CAST #3

A

STRIKE ZONE

Reel in and cast again, this time a shorter cast, and repeat with successively shorter casts until you are starting your drift only ten or fifteen feet from shore. Then move downstream a dozen paces and repeat the routine until you've explored the entire stretch of water where a steelhead might be found. Virtually every square inch of bottom can be explored by using this casting pattern when you're mooching a bait. You will need to make perhaps a half-dozen trips from head to tail of the riffle, on each trip making your casts from slightly different spots on the bank.

Each glide or riffle you fish will have its own characteristic currents, its danger spots, its deep holes and shallows. As you fish you will be able to form a pretty good mental chart of the streambed, you will learn where it is clear and your sinker will dance merrily along, and you will also learn where you must lift the tip of your rod a bit to avoid getting snared by the snags. More importantly, you will learn the paths the steelhead take as they travel through the section of the stream you're fishing. Like all wild fish and animals, the steelhead is guided by instinct rather than reason. It follows a fairly well-defined route through each section of water it passes in its upstream travel, and once you've learned to put your bait on that route, you're ready to repeat next time around.

This is one reason why many veteran steelheaders like to fish only one or two riffles of two or three streams in the course of an entire season. Over the years, they've learned precisely where to cast on each of the riffles they favor, and when there are fish in the water, they'll probably take them. Fishing alongside Dutch Neilsen in Eulathorne Riffle on the Klamath one autumn day, I watched him take a half-dozen steelhead in quick succession with a cast only about fifteen feet long and from a stretch of water no longer than my arm. Dutch had been taking fish from that spot for over ten years; he knew to an inch where to cast and how far to drift and how to coax his line along the productive current. Needless to say, I marked the spot for my next trip to that riffle, and after a little experimenting was rewarded by finding the path Dutch had revealed.

Steelhead will generally hit a drifted bait with a solid strike, and will strike single salmon eggs much harder than they do roe clusters. You will seldom have to set your hook when fishing single eggs; you will almost always have to set your hook when using clusters. When you are drifting clusters of roe, and your line comes to a stop or even hesitates momentarily, twitch your rod tip upward a few inches. You may be striking at a false alarm, a bigger-than-usual rock that has slowed down your sinker's progress, or a waterlogged branch that has caught your line or terminal tackle, but it's better to risk a snag-up than to miss a fish. Because roe clusters are big, it takes a steelhead a few seconds to get them in its mouth; by the time you feel its tug, the fish may have discovered the hook and spit out the bait. So, strike when your line stops moving, and improve your chances of connecting.

Unless a river is unusually thick with steelhead, mooching a bait is generally more productive than plunking. The drift fisherman carries his roe cluster or single egg to the fish; the plunker must wait for the fish to come to his bait. Which method of bait fishing you elect to use is partly a matter of personal preference, partly one of geography. On the Pacific Coast, bait fishermen who favor plunking usually like to work the slower waters near stream-mouths and the lagoons. In the Great Lakes region, plunkers not only find good sport offshore, in the waters of the big lakes themselves, but in the lakes or lagoons that form the outlet of so many rivers. Productive waters of Lakes Michigan, Superior, and Huron often extend as far as a mile or more offshore and up to a mile on either side of rivermouths; there is almost always good steelhead fishing during the spawning runs at piers and breakwaters, usually as close as 60 to 75 feet off the water's edge and often much closer inshore.

If you are going to use the plunking technique anywhere, in lake, stream, lagoon or offshore in big water, patience and advance planning are the two keys to success. When going into hitherto unexplored steelhead waters, it's not time wasted to survey the stream first and make a mental map—or a sketch on paper, for that matter—of the spots where bait plunkers are working. Later on, you can return to these places with pretty fair assurance that you'll be casting to productive areas.

There's little difference between rigging your terminal tackle for plunking or drifting. You'll need a bit more weight to hold your line in the current and your bait in one spot. Since there's a limit to the weight in which pencil sinkers are available, you might have to abandon the cinch and pencil sinker combination and go to a bell or pyramidal sinker, especially if the water is deep and the current strong. You will lose some lead if you make the switch, but by attaching the sinker with light-test monofil to the swivel-eye, lead should be all you'll lose.

You should, however, use a shorter leader between sinker and swivel, one not more than ten to twelve inches. Roe clusters have a lighter specific gravity than does water; they float, even with a hook in them, and if you use a leader that's too long your bait will rise too high above the streambed. This is true only of roe; shrimp and anchovies tend to sink, in spite of the current's lifting action. Single eggs are seldom productive when fished as an anchored bait; save them for drifting.

Make your plunking cast quartering downstream, if you're just aiming for the middle of the channel. If you're trying to hit a specific spot at one side or the other of the river, you'll have to do your own experimenting to get it there. Each bit of stream has its own characteristic currents, and nobody but the fisherman himself, on the spot, can determine how best to take advantage of them.

To anchor your bait in midchannel might take a bit of experimental casting. In general terms, you should drop your lead upstream from and beyond the spot on the bottom where you want it to come to rest. While the lead sinks, the current will be carrying it downstream and the line will be dragging the terminal tackle toward you. The current will also be putting a belly in your line, and this slack must be removed by careful, slow reeling-in until you feel the lead lift from the bottom. When your line is tight, there is no mistaking the gentle movement of the bait in the current that is telegraphed to you via your quivering rod tip.

If your rod tip does quiver, your line is either too tight or too loose. Either way, you're in trouble. If the line is too tight, your sinker won't hold the bottom; the current will move it, slowly and often imperceptibly, until you're no longer dangling your bait where you wanted it. If the line is too slack, the feel of a fish taking will be lost in the belly long before it gets to you and signals you to set the hook. When your line is at just the right tension, you'll be able to lift your sinker off the bottom by raising your rod tip an inch or less, and when the tip is lowered you will feel the sinker settle solidly into place once more.

When fishing quiet water rather than the streambed, put aside the Klamath Cinch in favor of a slip sinker. These are the oval weights with a center hole through which your leader is threaded; a rubber band wound to form a bulge in the leader below the sinker and 10 to 12 inches above the bait will give you the proper distance from weight to hook for easy casting, and will allow your bait to ride about the right distance from the bottom. When the steelhead takes, the line or leader will slip without resistance through the hole in the sinker and will keep the fish mouthing the bait until you have time to react to the strike.

Once you have your bait placed where you want it on the bottom, it's up to you to keep in touch with what's happening down there, and keeping in touch means quite literally that you must rely on your fingers touching the line. With the rod in one hand, hold a bit of line firmly between the fingers of the other hand, ready to lift the rod tip the few inches necessary to set your hook firmly when you feel a feeding fish. Steelhead are individualists; no two ever take an anchored bait in precisely the same way. In this they are unlike other game fish, which have consistently predictable habits of hitting a baited hook.

There is, of course, a pattern to the manner in which steelhead take roe baits. The key word is gentle. Because of this, plunker fishermen miss hooking a lot of steelhead. They will make a cast, get their bait placed to their liking, then lean their rod in a holder or a forked stick, or against a boulder, while waiting for a fish's nature to take its course. A good percentage of the time, this is done to give the angler a chance to gather up some driftwood and build a fire, a project certainly blameless and usually necessary. But he's not holding the rod when the fish takes, he's apt to be several yards away, and by the time he's noticed the bobbing rod tip and run to investigate, the fish is apt to have moved on.

A steelhead's normal approach to a roe cluster is gently hesitant, so gentle that if you're distant from your rod you may not ever see the telltale signs of the fish investigating. Down at the business end of your tackle, the steelhead will be hanging in midwater, mouthing the roe cluster very softly, chewing it to crush the individual eggs and extract the juice they contain. Bait fishermen call this "milking the roe," and the more honest among them admit that they can't always tell when it's happening, even if they're holding the rod.

It's hard for a fish to milk the roe without betraying its presence to a finger holding the line, though. Your best insurance against missing a chance at a fish is to keep in touch with the bottom of the stream by keeping a finger on the monofilament. When you feel anything at all causing your line to twitch or vibrate, raise the rod tip a couple of inches. This is as far as you need to move the rod. If the fish has the roe cluster in its mouth, you'll sink the hook in its jaw. If the cluster isn't fully inside the steelhead's mouth, and moves away only an inch or so, the fish is inclined to follow and mouth the bait still more, giving you a second chance to set your hook. However, when the bait is suddenly yanked away a foot or more, the fish either gets suspicious or discouraged and goes on about its main business, which is to swim upstream to the spawning bed.

Occasionally, a cruising steelhead will strike a plunked bait hard enough to hook itself, but this doesn't happen as often as it does when you're drifting. The angler who doesn't strike quickly at the first sign of action is the fellow who will spend most of his time rebaiting his hook instead of playing and landing fish.

Most steelhead streams contain both small trout and half-pounders, which you already know are immature steelhead waiting to go to sea. These little nuisances are active in their feeding habits, and will nibble away at your bait, since the clusters are too big for them to gulp into their small mouths. Each nibble will get your spirits up, and keep you in that happy state of about-to-get-a-strike jitters. After a while, you will learn to distinguish the light tapping of the small fish from the gentle but positive tugging of a taking steelhead. Until that difference has been learned, you'll make a lot of false strikes—another good reason for moving your rod tip only the minimum distance required to set a hook in a real fish.

About the only difference between fishing roe clusters and shrimp or anchovies in plunking is the size hook you'll use. As already noted, a light wire hook will work best in combination with these solid-flesh baits, they will be torn less when being threaded on the hook and thus will stay on longer. Unless you have very small shrimp, split them lengthwise and impale them on the hook by working the barb into the shrimp from the shoulder; cover the hook completely, all the way to the eye. Weave the hook in and out of your anchovy fillets, leaving the barb exposed. Fish these baits just as you would roe clusters.

Use the absolute minimum weight required to keep your line down and your bait on the bottom when using shrimp or anchovies. The taking steelhead likes to test these baits before swallowing them; the fish will pick them up from the streambed and move them perhaps six or eight inches before taking the bait. Too much weight will end business right there.

So far, we've gotten the fish to the striking point, but haven't played or landed it. Assuming that you're using spinning gear, or at least a reel that has an adjustable drag, set that drag to offer about two-thirds of the resistance you'd normally set it for—and then keep your hands off the drag. Don't be afraid to give line to a steelhead; more fish have been lost by anglers trying to horse them or to stop their runs than for almost any other reason. You're in big water, heavy water, and the steelhead's instinct tells it to use the current. His long runs will be downstream, so that you're forced to fight both the fish and the water.

Let the fish have its head. Follow it downstream, along the bank, when you must. There will be times when the steelhead will stop and dog the hook, hanging in one spot, and this will give you the chance to gain a bit of the line you've lost. Don't be in a hurry to bring the fish to the bank. The steelhead's mouth isn't especially tender, and most fish taken on bait are hooked solidly.

If you make the mistake of trying to land a steelhead too quickly, before it's thoroughly exhausted, turning on its side on the surface, you might be in real trouble. Steelhead have amazing stamina and reserve. A partly tired fish brought into bank and feeling the sand on its belly can take off on a tackle-smashing run, just at a time when you're not prepared. Your line is short, your rod at a low angle to the stream, and you've lost the leverage that's made it possible for you to hold the fish in the first place. That fish you thought exhausted will surprise you by setting out on a run you can't stop, and you'll wind up with a broken line or leader instead of a gleaming steelhead in your hands.

So, be patient. Tire the fish completely, and when at last you bring it into the shallows at your feet, and halt its last desperate run, there will be no hitch in the final few seconds of action. With your line reeled in until it is no longer than your rod, the rod itself held high and at the vertical, take four or five steps backward, sliding the fish from the water onto the graveled bank. Drag it well back from the water, and don't stop yet to admire it. Put your rod down and get to the fish at once, before it flops back into the stream. Slip your fingers into its gills, kill it quickly and cleanly with a blow of a rock at the base of its head. Hold it up to admire, as the crimson blush begins to fade from its sides. Then bait up again, and see if the steelhead's twin is waiting for you in the cold water from which your first prize came.

One or two more thoughts about bait fishing. While it is not regarded in steelhead country as in some other places as being akin to matricide and child-beating, there is a style of baitless fishing that anglers hold in low esteem. This is snagging. Along steelhead streams there are barriers which form shallow pools in which steelhead often hang thick, waiting for the time to jump the barrier and continue upstream. A heavy line, rigged with a big sinker and a bare oversized treble hook, will, when dragged at high speed through these pools, snag fish in the back or belly and lay them on the bank in seconds.

Illegal in California, Oregon, and Minnesota, snagging is permitted in designated areas in Washington, with area and seasonal restrictions in Wisconsin, and is allowed without restrictions in Michigan. The latter state originally legalized snagging as a method of harvesting an oversupply of spawning coho and chinook salmon, which had returned to the streams in such unexpectedly large numbers that they created a disposal problem. Inevitably, since steelhead use the same waters as salmon on their spawning runs, they, too, became prey to snaggers. On a November day in 1972, I watched Bernie Halverson take four fine fish from the upper Muskegon River; all four bore the unhealed scars of snag-hooks.

Snagging is, of course, a method used by poachers and meat-takers rather than fishermen. It is a throwback to the old days when fish were harvested with a pitchfork to be salted down for winter. You may at some time or other accidentally snag a fish while fishing with legal tackle by legitimate methods; the game laws in all steelhead states require that such fish be released.

Anglers in steelhead areas do not equate bait fishing with snagging; most of them use bait at some time during the year, since given the character of the rivers it's often a choice of fishing with bait or not fishing at all. And the ultimate test of sportsmanship is the tackle, not the lure. If your terminal tackle is light enough to give the fish a sporting chance to break free when you apply too heavy a hand to rod and reel, you have met the test.

Fishing is a sport where a man pits his wits and frail equipment against the instincts and muscles of a fish, not a matter of subduing a fine fighting fish on tackle from which he cannot possibly escape. If you take a steelhead weighing six to eight pounds on a ten-pound test leader reduced in strength by knots to the fish's own weight, you have earned your fish and the thrill it's given you.

6

The Steelhead and Lures

Lure fishermen take between 65 and 70 percent of all steelhead caught, winter and summer seasons combined. There are several good reasons why this statistic is valid. The figure, by the way, is purely unofficial, not the result of a formal survey made by one of the polling organizations. It is my own figure, based on observation, and on discussions with game wardens, guides, tackle shop operators, and others in a position to come up with a very accurate estimate.

Sheer preponderance of numbers is the chief reason why lures account for so many good steelhead. There are so many more anglers who follow this style of fishing than those who favor bait or fly that even if every lure fisherman on every steelhead stream was a bumbling incompetent, unable to tell his rod butt from a riffle, lures would still take more fish than all other types of angling combined. And lure fishermen aren't bumblers by a long shot. The best of them take pains to familiarize themselves with the habits of the fish and characteristics of the waters, and experiment knowledgeably with sizes, colors, and shapes of lures and different styles of presentation. Those who do this take more fish than the lazier anglers, but even the fellow who just plops any kind of lure anywhere and retrieves it willy-nilly has a fair percentage of success.

Other reasons account for the dominance of these creations of shaped metal and moulded plastic and explain why so many fishermen prefer lures. The lure is a lot less trouble and a lot cleaner to use than bait, and does not have to overcome the legend of unsuitability woven around the fly. This legend is just that, of course, as will be seen in a later chapter, but right now the subject is lures. The casts required in lure fishing are easier to master than those called for with either bait or fly; casting with terminal tackle rigged for bait is a clumsy proposition, and fly casting is an acquired skill requiring practice. Today's spinning tackle has closed the gap between veteran and novice where lure casting is concerned.

Purely aside from these reasons, the lure would still predominate in steelhead fishing as it does in most other freshwater angling, because the lure is particularly and peculiarly American. From the day when some unknown genius—reputedly, a doctor in Connecticut—noticed how fish rushed to strike a silver spoon he'd dropped accidentally from a rowboat in clear water, the lure has been the pet of American fishermen.

From the misty day in 1830 or 1840 when the anonymous doctor noted the attraction glittering metal has for fish, anglers and tackle-tinkerers both amateur and professional have concentrated on developing the lure. In all its centuries of fishing history, England has produced only two original lures of note; the Scandinavian countries perhaps three. Europe generally paid little attention to lures until just before World War II, and most of the lures developed there date from 1940. Americans began developing the lure a hundred years earlier, and this development has never stopped; thousands have been invented, and new ones appear every year. A lot of them take steelhead.

Clumsy tackle kept steelhead lure fishing in a retarded state until the spinning gear boom that began in the late 1940s. Before that time, lure fishermen on steelhead rivers used heavy fly rods and multiplying bait-casting reels and heavy braided silk lines that soaked up water like a sponge. The long rod was needed to get distance in casts that were impeded by the dragging lines; it was a marriage of basically incompatible types of tackle, and like all shotgun weddings, not an especially happy one. But, men who acquired skill in using this combination still cling to it, and though most of them now use monofilament lines, they can shoot lures tremendous distances with great accuracy.

There is really no difference between the tackle required for lure fishing and that used for bait fishing, as described in the preceding chapter. You will still need a rod nine feet or more in length, a heavy-duty spinning reel that can spool 200 yards or more of 15- to 20-pound test monofilament or Micron, or a suitable bait-casting reel similarly loaded. If you are fishing the heavy waters of the Pacific Coast, you will also need a few Klamath Cinches and a big handful of pencil sinkers. These weighting aids are not needed in the slower-moving waters of the Great Lakes streams. In all but one or two rivers, metal lures will hover close to the bottom, while in West Coast streams the same lures would plane up to the surface. Even the buoyant plastic-bodied lures that must always be weighted in western rivers can be fished without lead being needed to hold them down in the gentler currents of the inland streams.

It's when we come to the selection of lures that the fun begins. There are many veteran steelheaders who will use only one or two types of lure, regardless of weather or water conditions. On overcast days or days when the streams are still clearing, they may go to a silvery lure rather than one in copper or gold hues, but this is the extent of their switching. And these men catch fish, big fish, consistently, because they are artists at the manipulation of their favorites. Their success comes because of their skill rather than through any virtue intrinsic in the lure they favor. Any angler fortunate enough to fish with these experts can learn a lot by watching them and listening to them, but not all of us are capable of such single-mindied concentration. The average fisherman is better off carrying an assortment of lures to the river.

Steelhead lures fall into two big families, each having two sub-divisions and a number of minor classifications within the subdivi-sions. In spite of the claims of manufacturers that such-and-such lure is unique and infallible, and in spite of patent laws that are supposed to give inventors protection against design piracy, no popular lure escapes imitation. Sometimes it seems only a matter of weeks be-tween the appearance of a new lure and others that copy it almost exactly. But in spite of this proliferation, the basic classifications still apply.

In one big family group are all the thin-bladed metal lures, sub-classified as spinners and wobblers and with other subclassifications that we will meet later on. The second family group is made up of the thick-bodied lures; its subdivisions are the chubby ones such as the ancestor Cherry Bobber and its descendants, and the elongated, thin ones like the Flatfish and its imitations. Of all the hundreds of lures I've used and looked at, I have yet to find one that cannot be fitted into one of these families and their subdivisions.

Since the sage has quite correctly pointed out that the journey of ten thousand miles begins with a single step, we might as well take our first step by moving to the spinner group of thin-bladed lures. Then, as we travel, we'll meet a representative cross section of the others, enough to give you an idea of what they are and how they can be used to your advantage in attracting steelhead.

Because it's the granddaddy of them all, and still the prime favorite of lure fishermen, let's start with the Colorado Spinner. This is the spinner predominantly favored in steelhead country. Though some-times found in oddball assemblies, the typical steelhead lash-up of the Colorado is a size #2, #3, or #4 blade on a three-inch shaft with several red beads fore and aft of the blade, for spacing, bearings, and subsidiary attractors. This typical assembly ends in a treble hook which may be as big as #2/0 or as small as #4, depending on the fisherman's whim. This is what about 100 percent of all lure fishermen will drag out of their tackle boxes when asked to show their favorite spinner. A few will prefer the Indiana blade, which varies only slightly from the Colorado.

Shaft length of the Colorado spinner assembly will be an almost uniform three inches, give or take a fraction, and red or orange beads are also standard. It's when we come to the blade's finish that the individual fisherman gives his imagination the greatest leeway. There are blades of copper, gold, silver, bronze, brass, and chrome; there are half-and-half combinations, copper on one side with silver on the other, or the lower half of a blade will be one of the yellow-hued finishes and the top a silvery finish; and so on to infinity. A little quick arithmetic will show that by juggling nothing but the metal hues already mentioned, without even adding a drop of paint, there are 578 variations possible. Each of these can be a plain finish, or hammered, etched, engine-turned, brushed, or engraved. This gives us a clearly impossible 2800-odd combinations of hue, and when multiplied by the number of sizes possible to use, the total number of just Colorado spinners available approaches that of the number of dollars in the national debt.

Returning from the realm of fantasy, the most practical and experienced lure fishermen are content with a Colorado spinner assortment that includes perhaps a half-dozen combinations of finish and size. The most commonly encountered sizes are #3 and #4; the most popular finishes are hammered and plain silver, silver face with copper, gold, or bronzed or brass backs; or with two-toned blades divided diagonally, one half the blade a silvery tone, the other half one of the yellow-hued finishes. There seems to be a pretty even division of angler preference; no single color or combination of colors dominates.

Incidentally, I've seen two extremely fancy sets of spinners used, the property of fishermen who will be nameless here, as much to discourage their ostentatious flaunting of wealth as to spare them from becoming the butt of envious jokes by their poorer colleagues. One of these gentlemen owned a set of sterling silver spinners with his name engraved on them, the other had two made of fourteen carat gold set with tiny rubies. They used the spinners, too, but the fancy jobs took no better or bigger fish than did spinners of baser metal whose snagging on a riverbottom would not bring on the anguish that must accompany the loss of such deluxe lures.

Whether of gold or silver or baser metals, all spinners will take steelhead most of the time. There is none which is universally effective or unusally deadly in the hands of the average angler; the effectiveness of any spinner depends more on the skill of the angler manipulating it than on the metal from which it was made. Action seems to be the important factor rather than color or blade size. It's true that sometimes steelhead will pass up the big blade offered by one fisherman only to hit the tiny spinner being fished by his next neighbor along the bank, or vice versa, but I've seen really skilled spinner-users take fish with big blades while everybody else was getting strikes on tiny spinners—and, again, vice versa.

Several fishing lessons I've been given, though, have convinced me that action and manipulation are the key to success when fishing with spinners. One of these lessons is especially vivid in my memory; I got it on the Klamath River's Blue Creek Riffle years ago, when I was first beginning to learn that happy stretch of water. There were four of us; we had beached our boat to fish on the bank, since four lure fishermen trying to operate out of a relatively small craft find things getting a bit crowded. The first cast was made by Frank Watters, whose line was equipped with a #3 Colorado spinner. Frank got an immediate strike, so the rest of us put on #3 Colorados and started fishing. Frank's fish, incidentally, had tossed the hook after a couple of good leaps.

In what seemed at the time to be just a matter of moments, but was probably something like twenty to thirty minutes, everybody but me had either landed a fish or had lost one after a strike. Harry Hammond was fishing next to me along the bank; after he'd landed and released a four-pound steelhead to let the fish grow up, he walked up to where I was casting and watched me for a moment. Diffidently, he suggested that I work my spinner more slowly.

I handed Harry my rod and asked him to demonstrate the speed he recommended, but the demonstration was cut short. Harry's first cast, in the same stretch of water I'd been working so hard, brought in a six-pounder. The fish hit before the spinner had traveled six feet along the bottom. He released the fish; it was under the eight-pound minimum we'd agreed would be the smallest fish we'd keep. Then he handed me the rod, saying with a grin, "They're in there, all right. Go on and catch a few."

Taking the rod, I tried again, but after another quarter hour of diligent casting had still gotten no action. Meanwhile, the others of the group were having a ball, and Frank and Elmer Meyers had both taken keepers. I called to Harry and asked if he felt like giving me another lesson. He put his rod aside, took mine, and this time managed to make three demonstration casts and retrieves before a slim five-pounder grabbed the hooks. I thought I'd gotten the idea, but still more casting proved I still had something to learn. Harry cheerfully took up school again, and after watching him make a dozen casts, I finally spotted the difference in our styles. He'd been holding the rod tip low, almost touching the water, while I'd been working my retrieves higher and faster.

Just what difference this made to the spinner's action underwater, I still am not sure. I only know that when I started imitating Harry, I began to get strikes. Within a half-dozen casts I was onto a roe-heavy female that was just a quarter pound short of our self-imposed eight-pound minimum. For the remainder of the afternoon, I took fish as consistently as did the others in the quartet, but only when I worked the spinner so slowly that it was just hanging in the water and only when I held my rod tip very close to the surface of the stream. During those periods when I experimented with a faster action, holding the tip of the rod high, I went without strikes.

Remember, Harry and I were using the same tackle, standing in the same spot, casting into the same stretch of water. The only difference was in presentation of the lure. This may not prove anything to you, but it does to me. It emphasizes the importance of varying your style of offering your spinner to the steelhead if your first casts don't bring strikes. On other days on Bear Creek Riffle, the fish responded to a faster-moving spinner, and the angle at which the rod was held didn't seem to matter.

Never mind figuring out the "why" of a steelhead's habits on any given day, just fish in different styles until you've learned the "how" for that particular time and place. You may never know why, to your complete satisfaction; I haven't figured out why the fish wanted a certain specific style of presentation that day on the Klamath. I did figure out, though, that if what I was doing with my lure didn't please them, it was up to me to try something new, not wait for the steelhead to change their minds. Fish can be very stubborn, sometimes, in expecting the angler to accommodate them.

There are several ways in which you can vary your presentation when lure fishing; it allows the angler more options than either bait or fly fishing. You can let the current tumble your lure at its own speed, or slow down its pace, or let it go downstream in jerks. You can vary the angle of your rod tip, which will affect the way in which your spinner blade revolves. You can cast upstream, quartering upstream, cross-stream, or downstream, each of which results in a different type of lure action even without you changing the pattern of your retrieve. And in each of these casting directions, you can retrieve at different speeds, still further varying your presentation to the fish. Sooner or later, you'll hit on the style that appeals to the steelhead at that time and in that place. Then, you've got it made, at least temporarily.

Before getting sidetracked, we were investigating spinners in general and the Colorado spinner in particular. The detour doesn't represent any lost effort, for what applies to the Colorado applies equally to other members of the spinner family. It's not really a big family; the Colorado is its best-known member, then the Indiana and the willowleaf. There's also the kidney-shaped Canadian blade, which is used principally in opposed pairs in trolling rigs, since a single spinner blade of this type twists lines very badly. Though tackle makers have and still do come up from time to time with minor variations of the three basic oval-shaped spinners, the hard geometric facts are that their scope for change is extremely limited.

These limitations also apply to the weighted spinner jobs, the Metric, the Abu Reflex, and the Hep. Others in the family whose names you'll recognize are the Mepps Aglia and the Shyster, and there are others not as widely advertised. In their basic design, these are merely modified blade-and-bead rigs. Some have oval bodies of metal or ceramic or plastic; some have bullet-shaped or conical bodies. Some wear beads or feathers at their heads or tails, others don't.

Whatever their shape, whatever their action, all spinners will take fish—sometimes. None will take steelhead all the time. It's up to you to lure the fish into striking by varying your styles, just as a woman attracts you by varying her hair-do and makeup pattern. After all, it'd really be dull if everything stayed the same forever.

Somewhat more varied in its offshoots is the wobbling branch of the thin-bodied lure family. Like spinners, wobblers are available in an astronomical number of sizes and finishes and in a number of different shapes. The most common wobbler shape is that of a blunted oval, slightly larger at one end than the other, and with a concave form which gives the lure its characteristic erratically tumbling action, and its name. A few of the wobblers are more complex in form than a simple symmetrical concavity. They may be concave in the upper half, then go into a reverse curve like a mountain sheep's horn, or be stamped into creases that give them a faint resemblance to trimmed-down paper airplanes. A few are asymmetrical, a few thick and fairly flat of body, getting their action from bevels at either end.

Whatever their shape, they will wabble in the water when taken by the current, and this action will be even more pronounced when the lure is retrieved against the current—or in still water, for that matter —if you reel briskly enough.

Wobblers range in size from tiny one-eighth-ounce jobs no bigger than a thumbnail up to blades as big as a man's hand. For steelhead, the most effective size range seems to be from about ¾ up to two inches in length. Regardless of the trade name under which they're sold, almost all the oval-shaped wobblers stem in design from the Eppinger Daredevle, which was first of the wobbler breed to achieve universal recognition and is by far the most widely imitated. In addition to those of plain metal, available in all the combinations of metallic hues already noted for spinners, wobbling lures are commonly enameled, which makes your color choice still wider. They come in all shades from basic black to brilliant crimson, some striped, some polka-dotted, and some adorned with irregular blobs of color that might have been spattered on by a surrealist or abstractionist artist.

Because they were the first wobbling lures I used, I cling to the red-and-white barber-pole striped Daredevles that were almost a trademark of this lure in its earliest days. I fish them more often than I do the fancy or plain metal ones, and take fish with them, but suspect I use them more frequently out of habit than because I've found them better fish-getters.

Even in writing this, memory proves my point. I recall days on steelhead riffles when the fish would hit on copper, but not silver or gold wobblers, all of them being lures of the same size, from the same maker. I've also seen days when the metal-finished wobblers were barren of results, but those of red and white brought strikes. So, like all fishermen, I'll go on carrying a variety of sizes, colors and finishes in the wobbler section of my lure box, and suggest that you do the same, if only as insurance.

Like the Daredevle, most wobblers stay with the familiar spoon-bowl shape. In addition to the Eppinger lure there are the Kam-looper, Little Cleo, Wob-L-Rite, the Davis Hotrod, and a long list of look-alike, act-alike wobblers that have the same basic contours, varying only in their degree of convexity. Some have bucktail or feathers covering their hooks, and on most of them the treble hook attached with split-rings is standard. A few, such as the Johnson Bullet, have single hooks forged to their bodies.

Departing from the concave/convex shallow spoon-bowl shape are the Sidewinder, a sort of half spoon; the Gladding Super Duper, which has straight sides and darts rather than wobbles; and a handful of others. There are a few very heavy wobblers, slim ovals that get their action from deeply beveled ends; examples are the Acme Kast-master and Nesco Torpedo. Generally, these lures are heavy enough to be fished in most waters without the addition of a sinker. Another heavy lure is my own Deep Diver, which is not manufactured commercially. It is a miniature version of the flasher/attractor blade trolled ahead of bait by commercial fishermen. I make the lure out of heavy-gauge stainless steel, forming its simple curves over the head of an old carpenter's hammer. It is easily duplicated, using only a machinist's hammer and drill, and you are free to bang out any number you wish for your own use, if you'd like to try it. The lure finds bottom readily without extra weight being added, and works quite well on steelhead.

Quite naturally, there is a difference between the presentation of a spinner and a wobbler. The latter is most often effective when it is cast quartering upstream and allowed to sink to the bottom on a loose line. Then, as the line is tightened, the lure is allowed simply to tumble along the bottom. To vary your style, cast quartering downstream and as the lure swings across in the current make it tumble by hauling in a foot or so of line with your hand and releasing it quickly, letting the monofilament slip back through the guides. A quite different effect in the wobblers' underwater action is given them bv raising your rod tip high and bringing it down quickly to the horizontal, reeling in about half the slack created by the rod action as you bring the tip down.

Practically all the wobbling lures, like the spinners, will need extra weight to carry and keep them deep. Use the Klamath cinch for this, of course, but enhance the lure's action by giving it a longer leader, sixteen to eighteen inches. If you manipulate these lures properly to give them the tumbling action they must have to be effective, they're going to be hitting bottom more often than any other lure. This means you'll get snagged more frequently, and it will be the wobbler itself that's snagging, not the sinker. So, be prepared to lose more wobblers than you think you can afford, if you fish with them consistently.

Continuing to trace the lure family tree, we come now to the branch on which hang the thick-bodied lures. Some of these are indispensable to the steelheader, though they are a relatively new type. The ancestor of them all appeared in the late 1930s, and is credited with being the brainchild of a Seattle barber named Will Korff, who hung a treble hook on a red bobber of the type used in bait fishing for panfish. Logically, Korff called his creation the Cherry Bobber.

Korff discovered that steelhead hit his Cherry Bobber with frequency and gusto. It was, besides that, an easy lure to fish, since the bobber's buoyancy kept it floating at the end of its leader above the snagging rocks and crevices on the streambed. News of the new lure spread rapidly, and home-made Cherry Bobbers appeared, followed quickly by manufactured jobs as the tackle industry got the word. There are now roughly 1001 variants of the original, all with different names. The latest to appear is called the Oakie, a half-inch globe of translucent, fluorescent vinyl plastic with a hole through which the line threads. Water action causes the lure to slip down and ride on the hook-eye; colors range from yellow through orange to deep red. Like its grandpa, which is still being used, the Oakie is a good fish-getter.

Some of the Cherry Bobber variants are round, some oblong, some bullet-shaped. There are models incorporating a spinner blade fore or aft, and others fitted with wings of metal or plastic that give the lure a whirling action in the current. A few have wool or feather tails covering the hook, and the color selection begins with white and goes through the shades of yellow, orange, and red all the way to purple. Red remains the most popular.

A predecessor of the Cherry Bobber is the Hoh Bug; though it has never attained the widespread use or popularity of Korff's invention, it may well have been his inspiration. The Hoh Bug originated on Washington's Hoh River, and its history is obscured by the same mist that shrouds the origin of so many fishing lures and flies. Traditionally, the Hoh Bug is made from the roots of the alder trees that grow profusely around the stream that gives the bug its name. The Hoh Bug is not widely imitated, and retains its original oblate truncated shape and its original colors, a buff-toned yellow with green dots. It is used successfully in the streams around its home on Washington's Olympic Peninsula. but has not traveled far. While the Cherry Bobber is popularly supposed to imitate a cluster of roe, nobody seems to know what, if anything, the Hoh Bug imitates.

All the lures of the Cherry Bobber family are fished like the roe clusters they imitate: cast cross-stream and allowed to drift with the current on a taut line, weighted by a pencil sinker. Because these lures are lighter than roe they will rise higher above the bottom; a leader no more than eight to ten inches long should be used between sinker and lure.

A quick look at the thin-bodied plastic plug-type lures is all that's needed to disclose that most of them stem from Charles Helin's original and very highly successful Flatfish. Indeed, the Flatfish has come to occupy a prominent place in the roster of steelhead lures. Most popular of the variants is called the Guppy, and there is another called the Lucky Lady, among the imitators. All have a shape very similar to that of the original Flatfish, all are manipulated in the same style, and your choice becomes primarily one of size and color. In both small and large sizes, the most popular colors of the Flatfish-type lures are solid red, solid silver, yellow with red dots, and black with white dots, in that order. Heddon's Tadpolly comes in the same general color schemes, with the red-overcast fishscale pattern being very popular in the Great Lakes area. The Tadpolly, by the way, is one of the few buoyant-bodied lures contoured to run to bottom in even the swiftest currents. Handle its presentation just as you would a Flatfish and you will find the Tadpolly very good indeed.

In fishing this type of lure the most productive cast seems to be one quartering downstream. This puts the lure in the water where the current will swing it to the near shore in a relatively short arc and makes it necessary for the angler to cast more frequently and move more often in order to cover the water thoroughly. When cast from the bank, Flatfish-type lures must be given action by the angler. The most effective manipulation seems to be a "swimming" motion given the lure by raising the rod tip eight to ten inches and lowering it quickly, letting the lure drop back with the current.

Flatfish-type lures are also very effective in the still waters of lagoons and in tidal waters at the rivermouths when an incoming tide is reducing the speed of their currents. In these areas, troll the lure very deep from a very slowly moving boat, or cast across the current and then retrieve the lure just as slowly as possible. One of the big secrets of taking steelhead on the Flatfish-type lure seems to be the angler's ability to work the lure at minimum speed.

There is another method of using this type of lure that is very effective and very appealing to tired or lazy fishermen. It works only if you can get into position near midstream, so if you are wading its use is limited to those riffles or glides where shallow water at their heads makes it both possible and safe for you to wade far out into the stream. In a boat, you can anchor near the middle of the river, just above the head of the glide or riffle. Using enough weight to hold the lure on the bottom, let the current carry it downstream and keep it in the area a few yards below the riffle's head, allowing the current to provide it with its "swimming" action. This method has worked for me with pleasant consistency, and I once watched a woman angler fishing a silver Flatfish in this style from a boat at the head of the Rogue's Walker Riffle taking a half dozen good fish in less than three hours.

Any fisherman equipping himself for a steelhead season is going to be lost in the glittering array of lures the tackle stores offer, and it's a rare angler who doesn't go overboard in his selection. He keeps telling himself, like the chronic alcoholic, that "just one more" won't hurt, and before he's torn himself away from the counter he's staggering—not under a load of liquor, but a load of brass, silver and copper. When you begin looking, remember that steelhead streams have riffles as much as two miles long. The man who takes to those streams a heavier load than he can carry without strain is either sentencing himself to confining his fishing to a limited area or to lugging an excessively heavy load of metal. Either way, he's going to wind up being tired, frustrated, and unhappy.

Through the years, I've inspected the tackle boxes carried by several hundred veteran steelheaders and have paid attention to their lure assortments. One or two had reduced their stock to a minimum which allowed them to use a pocket-sized tackle box, but they were the rare exceptions. Even those who specialized in only a single type of lure generally carried several in every size, shape, and color in which their favorite was available. All of them, especially those who played the field, had loads far too heavy for their streamside comfort.

It's certainly difficult to reduce the needed lures to a number that can be carried in a pocket-sized box, but common sense dictates an assortment that will fit a box smaller than a boxcar. The only way to keep the number of lures you carry to manageable proportions is to pay close attention to basic lure formation and shape, as well as size and color. By ignoring the overenthusiastic claims of proponents of a specific lure and exercising a great deal of self-control, it becomes possible to assemble an assortment for your tackle box that will give you a choice capable of handling almost every streamside need. The assortment will include spinners, wobblers, bobbers, and Flatfish-type lures in representative sizes and colors, and will give you a tackle box that is portable without requiring that you hire a porter to carry it for you.

In this ideal assortment there will be two sizes of Colorado spinners in silver, copper, and gold, both solid colors and half-and-half combinations. There will be the same variety of wobblers, plus two sizes of wobblers in red-and-white barber-pole stripes. The box should contain a few of the weighted-body spinning lures in at least two sizes, and one or two of the oddball spinners and wobblers. Representing the fat-bodied family, you should have large and small Cherry Bobbers or their equivalent, and a selection of the Flatfish-type lures in the three or four most effective colors and in two sizes as well.

This is a total of about thirty lures, roughly half or one-third of the number carried by most of the lure fishermen I know. It still leaves room for you to add a few special favorites, or extras of the type you fish most often. Such an assortment will meet virtually all your requirements, and will go into a box neither too big nor too heavy to carry easily. As time goes on, you will undoubtedly add more lures, new ones, or extras of those you've come to consider most effective. You'll wind up with a tackle box weighing thirty pounds or more, and you'll lug it around until you notice that the shoulder on the side where you usually carry your box is getting lower and rounder than the other. This condition is known as fisherman's list, and it will grow progressively worse until you either do all your fishing from one spot or from a boat, or conclude that you're carrying too much tackle, and weed out the contents of your box. At least, that's how it seems to work out for me.

Even after you've assembled your ideal assortment, some of the lures in it will need individual attention. Just because you bought those lures in steelhead country is no guarantee that as they come from the shelf they're completely suitable for steelhead fishing. Few manufacturers operate their production lines with the steelhead's tackle-busting abilities in mind, and some of the lures will need slight modification before being offered to the king of freshwater fish. In almost all cases, the modifications are so easy to make that they can be done right in the store at the time you buy your lures.

Many spinners and wobblers have hooks too small or made of wire too light for steelhead fishing. It's a simple matter to work the original equipment hooks off their split rings and replace them with hooks made of extra-stout wire and of the proper size. Many tackle dealers in steelhead areas carry both spinners and wobblers in a hookless state, leaving the selection of hooks up to the purchaser. Even if these lures have hooks on them, don't be hesitant about asking for a swap; this is standard practice. You'll probably pay a few pennies' difference for the better hooks, but it's a good investment.

As a matter of practical fact, most tackle stores in steelhead territory are staffed by pretty good fishermen. They'll frequently call to your attention the fact that a spinner or wobbler you've picked out should carry heavier hooks, and their advice should certainly be followed. When a tackle store clerk or operator makes this kind of suggestion, he's not just trying to work a few cents more out of your pocket; he's genuinely interested in seeing you walk out with lures having hooks that will hold the kind of fish you'll encounter.

It's hard to fault those manufacturers who equip their lures with hooks too light for steelhead, because only a small fraction of the output from their production lines will go to steelhead fishermen. The case of the Flatfish is a good example. In its original version the lure was equipped with offset twin hooks attached by pin-snaps to screw-eyes in a wooden body. These were adequate to hold trout and bass, but steelhead fishermen wanting to use the lure virtually had to rebuild it by putting heavy-wire treble hooks on with split-rings and connecting all screw-eyes with copper wire. Thus modified, the

Flatfish could be used for steelhead without body and hooks parting company; the hooks still pulled free, but the wire held the hooks to the line or leader.

Word of these modifications trickled back to the Helin factory, and eventually a plastic version appeared in which heavy treble hooks were attached directly to the body with screw-eyes. In use, the hooks proved to be too small and the screw-eyes still pulled out of the lure's body when subjected to the bucking plunges and leaps of steelhead. It was not until a Helin executive hooked and lost several steelhead with the Flatfish that the present version appeared, with large, sturdy hooks connected through the body by a steel trace attached to the line-eye. Today's Flatfish is not only better for steelhead, it's more efficient for all fish, thanks to steelhead anglers having proved the shortcomings that existed in the original.

There's one precaution to be taken with all your spinners, wobblers, and other lures before using them on steelhead. Unless you always use a snap swivel at the end of your leader, put a split ring in the line-eye of every lure you own. Most spinners, for example, have a line-eye of small-diameter wire, the same wire used in the spinner shaft. When you knot your leader directly to this small-diameter wire, you create a weak spot; the wire will fray and cut monofilament ten times as fast as will the heavier brass used in split rings. The split ring is inexpensive insurance against ending a long fight by having your leader break from the friction of a small-diameter wire, and being left with a slack line while your fish cruises off with your lure still hooked in its jaw.

Getting that lure hooked in a fish's mouth depends, of course, on your ability to keep the lure down on the bottom of the stream as consistently as possible. Perhaps the most common mistake made by lure fishermen on steelhead streams is their belief that because a lure is made of metal, and metal is heavier than water, the lure will automatically sink. This assumption results in thousands of lost fishing hours every year, and is responsible for another erroneous conclusion drawn by unsuccessful lure users: that the steelhead doesn't respond to any offerings of glittering metal. In both these conclusions, they're wrong. In arriving at the first, they overlook the inexorable physical laws of motion; in reaching the second they fail to realize that a fish can't respond to something it doesn't see.

Steelhead do respond, and very gratifyingly, to lures that enter the zone in which the fish spends 99 percent of its time while in fresh water. This is the eight to twelve inches above the stream bottom. The steelhead's not going to change its bottom-hugging habits to accommodate an angler; it's up to the angler to put the lure down to the bottom where the fish will encounter it.

Lure design is based on the laws of dynamics that govern the behavior of an object in an element having a radically different specific gravity than the object itself. The same basic problems confront the man designing an airplane wing and the one designing a fishing lure: to create a surface with a compound curve which under motive power will cause the curves to provide a lift that will sustain itself in an alien element. Likewise, the plane's pilot and the lure fisherman have a common problem: to apply motive power in a fashion that results in the curved surface behaving as its designer intended.

Like the pilot, the fisherman can make the curved surface move up or down by varying the amount of power applied, but the strength of air currents in the case of the plane and water currents in the case of the lure affect the power requirements. The designer allows for the effects of normal currents, and when abnormal currents are encountered pilot and fisherman must be prepared to solve problems not anitcipated by the designers.

Most metal lures are designed to give their best action in the relatively light currents of small rivers or the calm waters of lakes. In very heavy currents, these lures tend to plane upward under the application of what would be normal power in lighter currents. This brings the lure to the surface; it may not break water, but will run only a few inches deep. The effect is that seen when a water skier is pulled by a fast motorboat; the skier sinks when the boat's power stops. In the case of lures, current force equals motor speed, and if the fisherman merely holds the lure stationary on a tight line, it will rise to the surface. There, he has about as much chance of hooking a steelhead as he would by casting into his bathtub. The remedy is to insert a Klamath cinch into his terminal tackle, allowing a leader fourteen to eighteen inches long.

When the steelhead does respond to a lure dancing in the water in front of his nose, the response usually takes the form of a very healthy wallop. There's a catch, though. Because steelhead will frequently approach a lure from the side, it is often very lightly hooked. The strike is the point at which most anglers give their rod a mighty heave in order to set the hook, with the result that a lightly embedded hook is torn free. This hook-setting reflex is responsible for fishermen losing about half the steelhead that strike lures. Always remember that when a steelhead first smashes your lure it generally hooks itself, and keep in mind that it might be only lightly hooked. When the fish is lightly hooked, there's not a thing in the world you can do about it. If you follow the angler's instinct and try to set your hook, your fish is gone immediately. If, instead of rearing back on the rod, you play the fish with all your skill and a very light hand, you've at least got a chance to land it.

A firm wrist and gentle, persistent pressure will increase the percentages of landing a lightly hooked steelhead. This not only keeps the hook embedded, but gives it a chance to work in deeper, or for the fish to chomp down on one of the other points of your treble hook. Your objective should be to keep your line tight, but not too tight, through all of the leaping, plunging action that follows the strike.

A great deal of restraint is needed to do this. It sometimes requires all your self-control to take the calculated risk of losing the fish by giving line, by dropping your rod tip when it jumps, and by playing the steelhead until it tires instead of cutting the fight short and horsing the fish in. This is what separates the men from the boys in steelheading. You never know how firmly or how tightly a steelhead is hooked by the way it strikes. I've had solid hits, with the fish taking out 60 or 70 yards of line in its first wild downstream dash, only to apply too much pressure and wind up with a slack line. A good rule is to assume that every steelhead hitting your lure is hooked lightly, and apply all your skill to bringing the fish in with as little pressure as possible.

One of the best demonstrations of the virtue that can lie in handling a hooked steelhead gently on occasion was given me by Ralph Fairbanks on the Big Manistee in Michigan. Ralph hooked a steelhead—a good one, as we could see when the fish broke water. After a couple of surface rolls, the steelhead submarined and Ralph fed line gently but firmly as the fish headed downstream. Sixty yards below the boat, the steelhead surfaced again, and from the angle of the rod and line it was plain that on its downstream run the fish had passed under a submerged log—of which there are many in this section of the river.

Ralph did not hesitate, but laid down his rod and pulled the boat over with the oars until we were just over the snag. The fish by this time was on a slack line. With the tip of a second rod, Ralph fished along the downstream side of the submerged log until he found and picked up the line from rod number one. Moving quickly, he cut the line holding the hooked fish and knotted it to the end of the line on the second rod, then very gently worked the knot through the guides and reeled in until he could feel the fish. Now, when the steelhead felt the hook and jumped we could see that the line was free between rod and fish. Ralph played the fish down until it could be netted, a 14¾-pound steelhead just beginning to show its crimson stripes.

This is not a technique recommended for use by a novice, or by any fisherman who expects to salvage every snagged fish every time. A percentage of the times you try this stunt, your fish is going to take off before you've knotted the free line to the line on the second rod. But a snagged steelhead is a lost steelhead anyhow, so keep the technique in mind for use when you're caught in a similar bind. More important, remember the lesson that can be learned from this incident: that you'll land more steelhead by playing them with a light hand than you will by horsing.

Once you've got a steelhead on the line, you're going to forget most of what you've read or been told about the best way to play it. After you've landed a few, the proper reactions will become instinctive additions to your angling memory and you'll do the right thing automatically. But to give you as much help as possible when you're first starting out, here are a few tips to try to keep in mind.

Fight a steelhead with your rod held high, almost at the vertical.

Play the fish from the reel, but take full advantage of the length of that cushioning rod tip's flexibility to keep on a persistent, gentle pressure. When the fish jumps, it will be a few seconds before the sudden increase of line tension will be fully effective, which gives you plenty of time to drop your rod tip to lessen the strain on your terminal tackle.

Above all, keep your hands away from the drag adjustment on your reel. Set the drag before you start fishing to a point well below that at which your line or leader might snap, keeping in mind that drag tension increases as your reel-spool empties of line. Learn to look on that reel, even if it does have a drag that's easily adjusted while handling the fish, as primarily a storage place for your line. In steelheading, man does not fish by reel alone; let your rod do the job for which it's intended.

In addition to the jumps there are a couple of other critical moments in your fight with a big steelhead. One of these is the time when a fish will reverse its mad dashes downstream and start upstream toward you. The instant you see your line starting to circle cross-stream, or feel the tension on your rod slacken, don't wait—start reeling in fast. Especially during the first minutes after being hooked, before losing its vigor as it begins to tire, a steelhead can swim upstream faster than you can reel in. You'll probably have to take a few steps backward in order to maintain a tight line. If you're already on the bank, this presents no problem, but if you're in hip-deep water with your footing uncertain, you just might find yourself suddenly sitting on the bottom.

When wading, head for shore just as soon as you're positive your fish is well-hooked. The steelhead will want to stay in deep water at this early stage in the battle, and you can afford to let it do this if your reel is well-filled and there's no danger of the fish getting into a spot downstream where the banks narrow and create excessively heavy currents. You're going to have to bring the steelhead into the bank sooner or later, if you're lucky or skillful enough to hold it, so the quicker you get on shore yourself, the better off you'll be. Then, if you find it necessary to run along the bank and follow the fish downstream, you can do so more readily than if you had to wade.

Perhaps the most comfortable steelheading—lounging in a streamside shack while waiting for a fish to take your plunked bait. This shack, on the Suislaw, is like many in the northern coastal area. Photo by Irv Urie.

Early-morning hours on a Pacific steelhead river—in this case, the Kilchis—call for warm clothes to keep the chill mist from penetrating.

Pacific streams that are roaring in winter lose their wildness in summer, and so do the fish. This is the Deschutes. Photo courtesy Oregon State Highway Commission.

But in the Midwest, good steelheading is possible in shirtsleeve weather, as here on Wisconsin's Bois Brule. Photo courtesy Wisconsin Department of Natural Resources.

Even veteran steelheaders like Bill O'Neal of Eugene, Oregon, can make mistakes on riffles they know well. Following a hooked fish, he stumbled into a hole. He got back to solid ground and landed the six-pound summer-run fish—but such accidents don't always end happily. Photos by Pete Cornachia.

A fine stretch of fast water winter or summer is Steamboat Riffle, on the North Umpqua. Photo courtesy Oregon State Highway Commission.

At Dam Hole on Oregon's Trask River, steelhead
hang waiting to jump the natural stone barrier,
and anglers line up to catch them.

A fresh-run 9-pound steelhead from the Kilchis. The tiny dark objects on the
body just above the vent are sea lice, a sure sign of a fresh-run fish.

Steelhead mating in a California stream. The female is the larger of the two fish on the nest, or redd. Four other male fish are visible around the nesting pair. Photo by Paul Needham, courtesy California Department of Fish and Game.

A jet of compressed air in the body cavity forces out a female's eggs without harming her. The extracted eggs have a higher percentage of fertility. Photo courtesy *Muskegon Chronicle*.

There's a legend in steelhead country that fishing is always good when mist is rising from the water. Maybe it's not that simple, but this angler on the Tillamook has one on.

It's also much safer. So don't let the first flush of battle drive out of your mind the need to start for the bank, and don't be afraid to give up some extra line if it's necessary to do so to get there.

As the fight draws to an end, another critical moment occurs; this is when the steelhead makes a last desperate run in an effort to escape. Even after you've tired your fish thoroughly and it's turning on its side, steelhead still have the reserve power to make this final desperation dash. Usually, it can be checked by dropping your rod tip to the surface of the river and letting the fish take out the few feet of line left between it and the tip. You might have to give a bit more line, easy to do unless you've succumbed to the temptation to tighten your drag during the last stages of playing your fish in order to snub it more tightly. If you're on the alert, though, the last run is easily stopped.

Now, once more, at the risk of being a bore: you're not going to do any business with steelhead unless and until you get your lure down to the bottom. If you don't feel the bottom regularly with your lure or sinker, you're not fishing where the fish are lurking, and they're not going to detour very far out of their normal paths to chase the lure. Bottom fishing means snags, and snags inevitably mean that you're going to lose some lures no matter how carefully you fish. You'll cut down on the quantity of lost lures by using the Klamath cinch as part of your terminal tackle, but even then, you'll lose some. Elmer Meyers, a veteran of 35 years of lure fishing in the rivers closest to his Klamath home, likes to remark that before he learned to fish a spinner he'd left over a thousand lures on the bottom of steelhead streams. Today, Elmer boasts, he gets angry with himself if he loses a half dozen in a year of fishing nearly every day.

So, be prepared to replace spinners, wobblers, Cherry Bobbers, or whatever type of lure you happen to be using. Carry enough spares to see you through your trips, especially if you're going to rivers where there's no handy tackle store where you can get replacements. Based on my own experience, I'd estimate that a fisherman who uses lures consistently has a 100 percent replacement factor over a three-year period. This means you'll be losing about one-third of your lures each season.

Don't begrudge the lures you do lose, whether they're left in the mouth of a steelhead too husky for you to hold or whether they snag on a sunken log or a bad bit of rocky bottom. After you take a few steelhead, you won't regret anything it costs to bring the fish into a position where you can slide it out onto the bank, a witness to the skill of your rod-wrist. This is the ultimate reward for your outlay of time, effort and cash—the visible proof that you've tamed and conquered a mighty fish by your own skill. The reward's worth all it costs you to experience it.

7

The Steelhead and Flies

On any steelhead stream you visit you'll have little trouble finding an old-timer or two who will say with complete and convincing sincerity that steelhead won't take a fly on that particular river. These grizzled veterans will tell you this even though from the point where you're standing talking to them a half dozen fly fishermen can be seen playing steelhead.

This misconception about a steelhead's refusal to strike fur and feathers is as firmly fixed in American regional folklore as the belief that swamp water will cure warts, that all politicians are by nature crooks, and that women with full lips, wide nostrils, and natural red hair are prone to sexual excesses.

Zane Grey, writing in the early days of the century, was perhaps chiefly responsible for this error of belief. Grey's pieces in magazines were widely read; so were his books, and he was overly fond of putting into print his sweeping statement that on only two rivers, the Rogue and the Eel, would steelhead take flies. Later writers, Roderick Haig-Brown notable among them, have told of their success in taking steelhead on both wet and dry flies, but it's the old story of the mistake always outrunning and keeping ahead of the correction.

Certainly fly fishing for steelhead was in the early days of the sport an uphill proposition. Not until the 1950s did technology catch up with necessity and make available to fly fishermen lines that would sink fast and hold bottom in heavy currents. Even when the first sinking lines did appear, they were so stiff and wiry as to be almost impossible to cast in the long-reaching fashion required on steelhead rivers. The retarded development of good sinking lines was just one factor that delayed the development of fly fishing for steelhead. Before E. C. "Pop" Powell invented the double-built rod in the 1930s—far in advance of glass rods, of course—rods heavy enough to be used for steelhead were heavy and clumsy affairs. Reels then available were light and flimsy, given to jamming and breaking.

In part, the blame for slow development of fly fishing for steelhead must be placed on the preconceived notions of the sport's pioneers. To give them credit, they were a dedicated and persistent group, but they had also been conditioned to think of fly fishing in terms of taking trout in inland rivers and lakes. They were preoccupied with the two things that are always in the minds of good trout fly fishermen: imitation of natural insects and presentation of the fly in a natural manner. Given these limitations, early fly fishermen in steelhead country found themselves frustrated when confronted with rivers in which there is virtually no natural insect life to imitate, and rivers with currents that make "natural" floats practically impossible. A lot of them simply gave up and turned to lures or bait.

Enough of them persisted to develop the art, however, and the anglers of today are reaping the rewards of their trials and errors. Fly fishermen on steelhead streams are steadily increasing in number. Today, about 60 percent of all steelheaders use flies occasionally, and about 30 percent fly fish regularly, with ten to fifteen percent devoted to fishing the fly exclusively. A lot of the "occasional" and "regular" fly fishermen don't use fly rods, of course. They fish their flies with spinning gear, slipping a water-filled plastic bubble onto the leader to provide the weight needed to make casts. But this is still fly fishing, regardless of the sneers of purists.

Actually, there are few purists on steelhead streams. The water conditions already described limit fly fishermen to so few good days on the water that even the most dedicated fly fisherman turns to other types of tackle to quell his steelhead fever. As an ex-purist, I can speak with a little authority on this subject. I enjoy taking steelhead on a fly more than I do on spinning gear; to me, the challenge is greater. But when the rivers are so murky that all a fly fisherman will get is casting practice, I'll leave my fly tackle at home, break out the spinning gear, and fish lures or bait, as water conditions dictate.

If you're beginning your fly fishing experience with steelhead, you're very lucky; you'll have less to unlearn than the fellow who broke in on trout and bass. Forget such things as imitating natural insects with your flies, making precise presentations to rising fish, casting so that your line settles gently on the water after your fly has hit the surface, and using the most gossamer of leaders in calm pools where the fish hang to feed. These niceties do not apply to fishing the fly for steelhead.

Of the good steelhead flies, only two or three imitate anything; precise presentation is unnecessary, on most streams in winter, it's next to impossible; only on rare occasions do winter steelhead rise to feed; your cast will be looping and sloppy by trout-fishing standards, with distance rather than accuracy the criterion; you'll use a leader heavy enough to hold big fish; and you'll pass up those calm, smooth pools and fish the fast water. What you will learn to do is to push a heavy line 70 to 90 feet into a crosswind or headwind; you won't consider it a mortal sin to tick water with your backcast; you'll let your line hit the surface with a heavy splash, followed by a second plop as your heavy wet fly sinks. You'll also learn that after your line is down, the current takes care of presentation, leaving you with nothing to do except hold the rod, follow your line with its tip, and pray.

A delicate touch or sense of feel isn't needed to hook winter steelhead, and you don't need to strike them. The fish comes to your sunken fly with mayhem in its heart and hits with a savage bounce that tightens your line at once and telegraphs the good news through the arc of your rod. In almost all cases the steelhead hooks itself by the fury of its strike, and no cooperation is required from the fisherman.

This is winter steelheading, and I make no secret of the bias I have in favor of winter as being the time to enjoy the sport at its best. However, the summer steelhead situation has changed drastically for the better since the middle 1960s. This is due to two main factors, the first being improved hatchery techniques that have increased the planting of summer-hatched fish to increase the warm season runs. Until man began helping nature this way, summer runs in all but a few streams were small and undependable. In some streams today, the summer runs rival the winter's for size. The bigger the run, the greater the number of mature fish that will be returning for second, third, and fourth spawnings, bigger and sassier on each trip they make back into fresh water.

Second of the factors chiefly responsible for summer steelheading's continuing improvement is another discovery made in the 1960s by a team of biologists of the Oregon State Game Commission. This research group, headed by Harry Wagner of Corvallis, found that hatchery steelhead, unlike wild-spawned fish, are not impelled to hurry to the spawning beds. The hatchery-bred steelhead seem to confuse the point at which they were released as smolts with the spot at which they should spawn, and hang in the vicinity of this release point for a while.

As a result, Oregon's policy is now to release hatchery smolts in areas accessible to anglers, and where stream conditions favor the fish staying around for a day or two on their return. What this means to the fisherman is quite obvious. Over a period of years the controlled release policy will become the equivalent to an angler's insurance policy almost guaranteeing good fishing. And, since summer waters tend to be much clearer, and currents calmer, the day will quite probably arrive when by using more delicate tackle the summer steelheader will enjoy the same challenge as that formerly offered only by the winter fish.

Certainly winter steelheading with the fly calls for tackle that's anything but delicate. Occasionally, in years of lighter-than-normal rains, winter streams will run clear. Then, the winter fly fisherman finds his big #2, #4, and #6 flies worthless, and steps down in size until he's using #10s and #12s offered at leader-length below the surface, on tippets with a three- or four-pound test. He'll land perhaps one fish out of every six under these conditions, but that one fish makes the rest worthwhile.

If your taste runs to shirtsleeve fishing, the Great Lakes area is the place to go, especially to the streams in Minnesota, Wisconsin, and Michigan's Upper Peninsula that empty into Lake Superior. In these northernmost rivers the water temperature remains in the range preferred by steelhead even in midsummer, and if the streams fail to produce, there is excellent offshore fishing. But go to these northern areas prepared for cool nights and some cool days, even in mid-summer. On the Pacific Coast, Oregon and Washington have improved and are improving the summer steelhead capability of their rivers. Check the stream-by-stream rundowns of both areas that are given in earlier chapters, but reinforce this information with inquiries before planning your trips to take advantage of the latest developments.

So, choose your season and your weapons, light tackle or heavy, and set out during the time of your choice, forewarned as to what you can expect to encounter. If you're addicted to using fairy rods and gossamer leaders, go out for the summer runs. If you want to test your skill to the utmost and are prepared to face uncomfortable weather, winter steelheading is your dish.

Most summer steelhead fly fishing can be handled with heavy trout-fly tackle; it's the winter fishing that takes special equipment. Let's concentrate on fitting you out for winter steelhead, and from its requirements you can readily determine what you'll be needing for summer.

Thanks to improvements in tackle technology, it's now possible to assemble a good winter steelhead fly outfit without hitting the bank account too hard and without having to build part of the gear yourself. In earlier years, about the only way you could acquire the proper tackle was to find the heaviest fly rod going, and then splice up a line with the weight and taper that balanced the rod and made possible the long into-the-wind casts this kind of fishing calls for. Now, everything you need can be found at a good tackle shop.

When you go looking for a steelhead fly rod, you'll be after one that's nine or nine and one-half feet long, having what's commonly described as "fast" or "dry fly" action. If you're new to the sport, this simply means that the power axis of such a rod is in the upper half to one-third of the rod, rather than having the action distributed evenly from butt to tip. This power axis can be found in any rod by raising its tip to the vertical and bringing your forearm—and the rod, of course—down sharply until both are horizontal. Stop the downward snap abruptly at that point, keeping your eyes on the rod. For fishermen's purposes, the power axis is at the point where the rod arcs in the most pronounced curve.

You might have to test several rods, unless you're looking at custom-made bamboos, to discover the one that's right for you. Do your initial testing with the rod unfitted, no line or reel, but don't stop there. After you've made a preliminary choice of several rods, test them further with the kind of reel you'll be using and a line that balances to the rod. Choosing a fly rod is a very personal matter, and you're the one who's going to be using the rod you pick out. I have friends who swear by their favorite fly rods, yet these rods often feel clumsy to me. My friends cast with them as far and as accurately as I do with my own tackle, and they have the same lack of enthusiasm for my favorites as I have for theirs.

In recent years many tackle manufacturers have come out with the so-called "ferrule-free" rods, a concept pioneered by Fenwick about 1962. These rods are supposed to settle the old controversy that began with the first fly rods, over whether or not ferrules put "dead spots" in a rod's action. I've fished with just about every kind of fly rod man's ever made, including three-section, two-section, and four-section rods, and rods that were made all in one piece. My observation has convinced me that ferrules have an adverse effect on rod action only if they are badly fitted. In plain words a rod will deliver the action built into it by its maker. A rod with bad action will have bad action whether it's got four ferrules or none at all.

Again from the fisherman's standpoint, about the only effect that well-fitted ferrules have on a rod is to increase its weight by so many fractions of an ounce. This by itself is of importance when using the big rods suited for winter steelhead fly fishing; those fractions of an ounce weigh pretty heavily on your casting arm toward the end of a long day's fishing. Many times, though, a rod weighing a quarter to a half ounce more than another one which has the same length and action will feel better in your hands. In such a case, disregard the weight difference and get that rod that is more comfortable for you to handle.

There are, I'm sure, many fine glass rods made that I've had no opportunity to use or test, and others of which I've never even heard. In listing the top-grade rods, it's not my intention or desire to be unfair to or to overlook any manufacturer. But from my own observations and experience, my use of a large number of rods by many makers, I would not hesitate to recommend the glass rods made by Fenwick, Silaflex-Browning, Orvis, Harnell, Herter, Berkeley, and Scientific Anglers, with their names listed at random rather than in order of choice. But, as I've mentioned earlier, a fly rod is a very personal piece of fishing tackle. The important thing isn't necessarily the name of the maker, but that the rod you select be right for you and be able to do the job you'll call on it to perform.

There are so many firms making good glass rods today that it's virtually impossible to be on familiar terms with all of their products. And, from my own use and observations, I've concluded that good-quality glass fly rods are now of such uniformity that you will not go wrong whichever of the better-grade rods you select.

Here, of course, lies the principal difference between glass rods, which are production-line products, and fine split-bamboo rods, all of which today are custom made. And I'm not talking about the imported cut-rate bamboo rods; all of these I've seen are uniformly sloppy in their action, cheaply fitted and carelessly wound. The only thing they have in common with custom-made split-bamboo rods is the material from which they are made. A good glass rod is infinitely preferable to a bad bamboo, so if you feel that the price of a top-quality bamboo rod is beyond your reach, by all means get one of the many good glass rods available at much more moderate prices than the bamboos.

There is a compromise, if you are reasonably handy with your fingers, enjoy tackle-tinkering, and yearn for a fine split-bamboo rod. Some of the custom rod-makers, fully aware of the high cost of their finished rods, offer split and glued bamboo sticks, usually with ferrules set in their plants, either as separate units or in kit form. Placing and winding on the guides, gluing on the grip and reel-seat, are easy jobs. Finishing your own rod not only teaches you something about the niceties of rod construction, but delivers for your use a good bamboo rod at a cost of roughly half what a shop-finished rod of the same quality would cost you.

Among the craftsmen who are keeping alive the bamboo rod, the best known are Leonard and Payne in New York; Orvis in Manchester, Vermont; Edwards in Mt. Carmel, Connecticut; Thomas in Bangor, Maine; and Winston in San Francisco. There are a few in addition to these, scattered around the country, who have earned good local reputations, but whose products have not yet been exposed to the acid test of nationwide use. A rod from any good custom maker will not only give you a great deal of pleasure, but will be with you a long time. I have split-bamboo rods in my wall-case that have been fished hard, season after season, for more than thirty years, and yet are still as fine in action and appearance as they were when they left the maker's bench.

Admittedly, my enthusiasm for good bamboo rods in this day of mass production is perhaps a reflection of an outdated fishing style. Put down my prejudice to the fact that I learned fly fishing when the only tool available for this style of angling was the bamboo rod, and my teachers were men who valued and appreciated good tackle. My prejudice does not close my mind to the glass fly rod; I own a couple of dozen of them, and use them regularly. They do seem to make me work harder on long casts than do bamboos, but fishermen who learned flycasting with glass rods and have never used any other kind have no trouble getting casts as long and as accurate with their glass rods as I do with my bamboos.

Your selection of a line, or lines, to go with your rod will be governed by the action of the rod you have picked out and by the style in which you plan to use it. There are three styles: with a conventional torpedo line, with a shooting head backed by monofilament, or with a lead core line with monofil backing. Regardless of the method you decide to use, there will be times when you'll wish you hadn't. If you're working wide water next to a fisherman using a shooting head or lead core line, you'll envy him for being able to make longer casts than you can with your conventional torpedo tapered line. If you're working next to a fisherman using conventional line, you'll envy him the ease of handling it gives him compared to your constant struggle with the monofil backing on your shooting head or lead core line. Let's look in detail at the advantages and disadvantages of each style, and the lines each one employs.

A nine- to nine-and-one-half-foot fly rod with action suitable for steelhead fishing will probably require either a WF-9-S or WF-10-S conventional line. These are the designations adopted in the mid-1960s by the American Tackle Manufacturers Association to replace the old letter system of line descriptions; under the letter system, these lines would be designated as GBF and GAF.

Without going too deeply into the technicalities of line specifications, WF-9-S (GBF) describes a line having three sections of varying length and line diameter. This particular line would taper for the first six to ten feet of its length from .030 inch in diameter to .055 inch; the .055-inch section would be ten to eighteen feet long, and then the line would taper to a diameter of .035 inch for the remainder of its length, and the total length of the line would be 100 to 105 feet. The precise length of each section of the line would vary according to the firm manufacturing it, as the key to precision in the ATMA system is the weight in grams of the heaviest 30 feet of line exclusive of tapering portions. In the case of the WF-9-S line, this section would weigh nine grams.

Translating the ATMA nomenclature, you would read: Weight Forward (line) nine grams weight in first 30 feet, Sinking (line). And, the WF-10-S line would obviously weigh one gram more in its forward section than the WF-9-S; from a manufacturing standpoint, the only way to increase weight of line within a given number of feet is to increase its diameter, so the heaviest section of the WF-10-S line would measure .060 inch. The S, for sinking, denotes that the specific gravity of the line is greater than that of water; if the line was designed to float, the letter informing you of this would be, not too surprisingly, F.

A conventional weight forward line will give you casts of 70 to 90 feet, even when the wind is in your face, if your rod and line are properly balanced and if you master the knack of shooting line from your left hand. Casts of this length shouldn't be considered unusual or spectacular, nor are they invariably necessary. Many riffles can be covered thoroughly with casts no longer than 40 to 50 feet; on others, and on a lot of the smaller streams, you can reach every bit of productive water with 30-foot casts. But the big rivers do require you to lay out a long line, and some anglers find it harder to get good distance casting the conventional weight forward taper than they do with a shooting head or lead core line backed by monofil. We'll get to these in a moment.

Shooting a long line isn't a difficult flycasting technique to use, if your tackle is in balance. The weight forward tapered line is designed to help you make long casts, and if you've done any flycasting you need only to adjust to the slower, lazier rhythm of the longer line and backcast and to learn the double-pull technique originated by tournament flycasting competitors. Pacing yourself to the rhythm is your own problem, and nothing written can help you there. The double-pull method of applying extra power to a cast basically consists of yanking your holding line with your left hand on both the backcast and the forward cast. There are a number of books on flycasting which describe the technique in great detail; another easy way to learn it is simply to watch a good fly fisherman working long line on a steelhead riffle.

When casting a weight forward tapered line, its heaviest section is always kept ahead of the rod tip; this is the working portion of your line. The lighter, smaller-diameter section is your shooting line, and it is kept in loose coils in your left hand or woven in figure-eight fashion on your fingers. The working line is picked up from the water's surface with a roll-cast, and brought up for the two or three false casts needed to give it momentum and establish the direction of your presentation cast. You will find that the double-pull, applied to backcast as well as forward cast when false-casting, adds tremendous speed to the movement of the line through the air.

It is this momentum that gives the heavy belly of the line the power to pull the smaller-diameter shooting line through the guides and across the stream when you make your presentation cast. If you have coiled or woven the line in your left hand properly, it will flow freely through the guides, while the loop traveling along the line's belly straightens and turns leader and fly to drop to the water. Today's sinking fly lines, most of them made of Dacron, submerge instantly and reach the bottom quickly, carrying your fly down to where the steelhead are moving.

In exceptionally deep or exceptionally fast water, it may be necessary to help your line sink. This is done after the forward portion of the line is already in the water, by making a short forward roll-cast with the shooting line and letting this cast pull an additional eight or ten feet of shooting line through the guides. This extra length of line can either be added to the coils in your left hand, or stripped from the reel quickly after you have released the shooting line.

As noted earlier, precise specifications of fly lines are left to the designers of the individual manufacturers, as long as the basic ATMA weight requirements are complied with. Manufacturers recognize that individual styles of casting as well as line-to-rod balance may make their lines either tip-light or tip-heavy in use, and almost universally follow the custom of putting a longer taper on the tips of their weight forward lines than may be needed. A few experimental casts will show you how much of this tip should be trimmed off to make leader and fly turn correctly. You may have to trim only a few inches from the tips of some lines, others will need a foot or more removed to obtain the proper action for your individual use.

You will also need to add backing to your forward taper lines; 100 to 105 feet of line isn't a great deal when a heavy steelhead running downstream in fast water starts your reel to singing. Many steelheaders go directly from the end of the shooting line to a fifteen- or twenty-pound test monofilament backing, using enough backing to make the reel comfortably full when the line is spooled on. I've found it helpful, though, in gauging the amount of line a fish has stripped off, to put a 50-yard length of hard braided nylon baitcasting line between flyline and monofilament. This type of line doesn't absorb water, and when you see 50 yards of twenty-pound test plug line melt away, exposing the monofilament, you know it's time to begin running downstream after your fish, before the sheer weight of the line you have out snaps your leader.

Shortly after the advent of dependable monofilaments, the "shooting head" came into use. Before these heads were manufactured, steelheaders learned to cut the shooting portion off their weight forward tapered lines and splice on 200 to 300 yards of twenty-pound test monofil, enough to fill the reel when the line itself was spooled on. Now, you can buy shooting heads ready to be spliced to the monofil; they are designated according to the ATMA specifications already given. Since the heaviest portion of a weight forward tapered line is all that works ahead of your rod tip, this enables the fisherman using a shooting head to get a slicker shoot, with less guide friction, and less weight for the working line to pull after it.

Very long casts are possible with the shooting head monofil rigging. Its disadvantage is that the length of monofilament you must handle while casting often results in snarls that foul when they hit the guides. To overcome this, many fly fishermen who use shooting heads loop the monofil between their lips when retrieving line, and let the shooting head pull the monofil out of their mouths on their presentation cast. This requires nice judgment in gathering the monofilament into coils that will not become tangled when released, but it's a knack that can be acquired with practice.

Holding the backing between the lips is actually easier and more practical than holding it in the left hand. Handheld, the wiry monofil often throws itself into snarls while your hand is moving while casting. Winding the backing into a figure eight in the line hand is better than trying to handle it in loose coils, but even this method quite frequently results in guide-catching snarls due to the monofilament's tendency to pack up in the hand. Controlling the shooting line with the lips sounds clumsy in description, but in practice it works out very well. However, learning to handle monofilament in this fashion is not something you would want to do while actually fishing.

Lead-core line is often used as a shooting head, in place of Dacron fly line. Lead-core line is available in diameters from .028 to .050 inch, and the middle range of these sizes makes it possible for you to build a shooting head that is very short, yet sinks fast. This is an advantage in brushy areas, where getting a long backcast is often difficult due to the foliage on riverbanks. The best lead-core lines are those having a sturdy nylon outer sheathing, which minimizes kink-ing and gives you a safety margin when the core breaks. But even the best of these lines will kink and the cores will break, making frequent replacement necessary and regular inspecting while fishing a wise precaution.

A lead-core shooting head is used just like one of Dacron, but you will find it necessary to use a heavier butt section on your leaders in order to make them straighten out and drop the fly properly. Just how much heavier your leader butt must be will depend on the diameter and length of the lead-core line you are using.

Many fishermen who favor Dacron or lead-core shooting heads have tried using them with spinning reels, in order to do away with the problem of gathering the monofilament backing in their line-hand or between their lips. While this does assure a snarl-free shoot, direct from the frictionless spool of the spinning reel, it complicates almost to the point of impracticability the final stages of playing and landing a fish. Because the spinning reel is designed and built with monofilament in mind, it does not handle the heavy, large-diameter working line satisfactorily. This presents the angler with a nice dilemma. He can either try to beach his catch with the 30 to 40 feet of working line still out, or he can coil it into one hand and hope that his reactions are fast enough to let him give line quickly when the steelhead makes its final dashes. Often, they aren't fast enough, and a lost fish is the result.

Clumsy as the method of gathering the shooting line or backing into the mouth may sound, it is by far the best solution if you want to use the shooting head technique in your fly fishing. It allows you to use a regular fly reel, and to play the fish from the reel during the entire fight. This is about the only way that a battle with a leaping, plunging steelhead can be won when you're using a fly rod. Always, always, play the fish from the reel rather than using your line-hand to strip in line and letting the line fall loosely into the water or boat. Water drag when wading, snarls when boat fishing, result in the disasters of broken leader and a lost fish.

Traditionally, a fly fisherman's reel is the least important piece of his tackle, for in small-water, small-fish fly fishing the reel is just a convenience, useful only for line storage. This is far from being true of steelheading. Here, the reel is a key item, its performance very important and quite often crucial.

Steelhead must be played from the reel in fly fishing. Many years ago, when California's Lake Almanor was seldom fished by anyone who did not live in its immediate vicinity, and when the lake produced rainbow trout ranging from seven to ten pounds in size, it was commonplace to fish with no reel at all on your fly rod. All fishing was done from boats, usually in water 60 to 80 feet deep, with the fly being retrieved from the bottom. Fly reels of the day, except for English imports such as the Hardy, would not accommodate the quantity of line and backing needed, so most fishermen took their line out on storage reels and uncoiled it, letting it lie loosely in the bottom of the boat. We had no trouble controlling the fish, big as they were, by hand-maintained tension on the line.

With this memory in mind, I tried using the no-reel technique when I first fished from a boat for steelhead. After a couple of tries, I went out and bought a reel big enough to handle a steelhead line and backing, for the steelhead's wild runs were impossible to handle with hand-tensioned line. Nor is it possible, when wading most streams, to risk letting retrieved line fall into the water. The current grabs the loop and sweeps it downstream, and when the steelhead starts a run, forcing you to give line, water drag on the loose loop more times than not will result in a snapped leader.

This need to play your fish from the reel makes your choice of a fly reel an important one. Extra-large capacity, once needed because the old lines and backing were very bulky, is no longer a requirement for a suitable reel. You are looking first of all for sturdiness in construction, simplicity in design, and dependability in performance. Elaborate and poorly made reels alike become casualties on steelhead rivers. Automatic reels are ruled out at once, because they lack line capacity, do not react in releasing the line quickly enough, and maintain too much line tension to allow the angler using them to handle a big, fast-moving fish. Geared reels such as are used for saltwater fly fishing are suitable, but tend to be heavy and clumsy. Reels using complicated and unorthodox brakes or drags—magnets and the like— have a distressing habit of suffering from the failure of some small component part when subjected to the strain of steelhead fishing. And I've seen bargain-priced reels literally collapse under this strain, with torn-out spools, broken-off handles, and cracked frames.

For many years the English-made Hardy has been the favored reel of steelhead fly fishermen. It is followed closely by the Beaudex and Pflueger Medalist, which run about neck-and-neck for second place. Today, there are also the Orvis reel, which is almost idenitical with the Hardy in design and is very well made; the Gladding Finalist, which adopted many of the Medalist's virtues when Gladding was joined by Pflueger as one of the Shakespeare subsidiary companies. There are also the new reels by Berkeley and Scientific Anglers, which appear to have been inspired by the Beaudex's time-tested design, and Feurer Bros.' Taurus fly reel, which can be used right- or left-handed. This is an attraction to many fishermen who alternate between spin fishing and fly fishing and have grown accustomed to thinking of the left hand as the reel-cranking hand.

All of these are single-action fly reels, light in weight in proporation to their line capacity, made of good-quality materials and carefully crafted. There are many other good reels capable of delivering the level of performance demanded by the steelhead fly fishermen that I haven't tested or inspected. But, in choosing a fly reel for your steelhead tackle box, keep in mind the indexes of quality materials, simple design, and good construction. Keep size in mind, too, though this is now a secondary consideration, thanks to advances in the production of lines and backing material less bulky than was once the case. A reel with a spool anywhere from 3¼ to 3¾ inches should certainly be adequate for your needs. I have a couple of fly reels with spools four inches and larger, and find myself using them less and less, in favor of the smaller, more compact, lighter reels.

One other bit of tackle remains to be examined: the leader. I have yet to see a correctly graduated commercially tied steelhead leader. A few have tippets that are far too light, but most of them can be faulted for having too-light butt sections. Leaders without enough body in their butt ends fail to transmit the power of the cast to the fly itself. They do not turn the fly over so that it settles to the water in a straight line from rod tip through line and leader. The fly drops back over the leader, sometimes over the line, usually forming a "wind knot." This one-loop knot cuts leader strength almost 50 percent, when it's pulled tight by the current. If it's not pulled tight, you'll have a tangled place in your terminal tackle and a fly that won't attract strikes.

Tying a tapered leader is no job; you can assemble a dozen in an hour by cutting all the strands at once and then getting on with the easy task of putting them together in the proper sequence with blood knots. You will have to keep in mind only one key: the butt section of your tapered leader should be no smaller than .005 inch less than the line to which it will be connected. With typical WF-9-S or WF-10-S, having .030 inch tips, use leader measuring no less than .025 inch.

Here again, ATMA specifications help you. If the maker of your favorite limp nylon monofil leader material doesn't mark the diameter on its spools, but simply states its test in pounds, you can translate breaking test strength into diameter in thousandths of an inch as follows: 50-pound, .028; 40-pound, .025; 30-pound, .023; 25-pound, .021; 20-pound, .0185; 15-pound, .015; 12-pound, .0135; 10-pound, .012; 8-pound, .011; 6-pound, .009; 4-pound, .075; 2-pound, .006. These are the standards for small-diameter monofils, which are by far the most common and widely used. They're also the best type to use for leaders as well as for fishing.

Since all but a couple of my steelhead lines have .030 tips, I start all my leaders with a butt piece of .025 monofil fourteen inches long. Then I go to eighteen inches of .023; eighteen inches of .0185; ten inches of .015; eight inches of .0135; and eighteen inches of .009 as a tippet. This results in a leader just over seven feet long, and since the blood knot used in making it up will cut the effective rated strength of the smallest piece of monofil by thirteen percent, I wind up with a leader of just under six-pound test. On days when the water is very clear, I'll replace the .009 tippet with .075 monofil. This may not fool the fish any more effectively, but it makes me feel very virtuous and painstaking. To be truthful, even this small change does seem to make a difference in the number of strikes in very clear water.

There's a good reason for the seven-foot-plus length of this leader, too. When I bring a fish in to beach, I still have a couple of feet of line beyond my rod tip, which lessens the chances for the knot joining the line and leader to jam in the tip-guide if the fish runs at the last moment and also reduces the possibility of the hard guide fraying and weakening the butt section of the leader when holding an almost spent fish close to shore for a few minutes, until he's tired enough to be beached.

This leader may not suit your style of casting or your rods and lines as satisfactorily as it does mine, but if it doesn't, experiment until you find a combination that does. Incidentally, the .009 tippet on the leader described will turn over quite easily flies up to #2. Generally, when I switch to a lighter tippet I also step down to #4 and #6 flies at the same time.

If this sounds like heavy terminal tackle to you, you're right. It is. I'm trying to save you from having to learn your leader lessons the hard way, as I did. Like most beginning steelheaders brought up on trout fishing, I had ample confidence in my ability to handle even the biggest fish on the most gossamer leaders. After all, I'd taken trout up to seven and eight pounds on leaders ending in 4x or 5x tippets, which when allowing for the reduction in strength caused by knots, makes them test at less than two pounds. Then there came a day on the upper Klamath, with a good winter run in and the water perfect for flies.

When the fish arrived, I was using a tippet testing four pounds. Within an hour, I'd hooked, held briefly, then lost six steelhead. I'd see my line straighten as the fish took my sunken fly, then feel an express-train-sized jolt in my rod-hand, and, perhaps one jump, then goodbye, fish and fly. After the fifth fish, I cut back the leader to its next section, which tested at five pounds, but that didn't seem to help. I told myself that I was striking involuntarily when I felt the fish hit, so watched my rod carefully on the next couple of strikes to avoid this error. It made no difference; there was the smashing strike, the jarring jolt, and the fish cruised contemptuously along, taking my fly with it. Six fish too late, I got the message and cut the leader back still more, until at last I was using an eight-pound test tippet. With it, I batted .500, losing one fish, but landing another, a beautiful, fresh seven-pounder.

Never underestimate the striking power of a steelhead. On days when they're in a smashing mood, which is most days when you connect at all, the only way to hold them is to use the heaviest tippets that are compatible with water conditions. Get into the habit of taking other precautions, too. Be sure all knots are tied perfectly, and that the leader has no frayed spots. Look at the leader after every few casts to make sure you haven't picked up a strength-reducing wind knot; this is easy to do on breezy days, for even the most expert fly fishermen will cast such knots when heavy steelhead flies get waterlogged and are blown back toward the line instead of straightening at the end of a cast. It's also important to check your hook now and then, especially when your backcast sails over a gravel bar or rocky riverbank; a ticked backcast under these conditions usually results in the loss of the hook point and barb.

We've now arrived at the shore of the last river to be crossed by the fly fisherman in assembling his tackle: the selection of flies. Because fishermen the world around run true to form, once they've been infected by the virus, nothing that I can say here about how few key flies you need carry is going to influence you to keep your fly box down to manageable proportions. Surprisingly enough, the number of universally effective steelhead flies is rather small, totalling no more than two or three dozen. To offset this, on every river you'll meet local anglers boosting one of the five or six strictly local patterns which they'll swear will take fish when other flies fail to get even a passing look.

Contrary to the widely circulated and generally accepted legend about all fishermen's lack of veracity, the claims made for these local fly patterns often turn out to be quite true. Even when the local favorites turn out to be nothing more than a minor variant of an established pattern, it's wise to try them. Adding them permanently to the number of flies you carry is another matter, but they'll probably wind up in your permanent collection anyhow, and might even prove to be effective some day on another river; this is how universally effective patterns are discovered.

Most of these locally famous flies bear the name of the river where they originated, or that of a local angler, or a town or landmark along the stream. You'll recognize such examples as the Umpqua

Special, the Stillaguamish Belle, the Orleans Barber, Brad's Brat, the Skagit Queen, and there are hundreds more. Those originated to cope with purely local conditions remain purely local flies; others that prove their effectiveness elsewhere go on to become residents in the fly box of almost every steelhead fisherman.

Jim Pray's famous Optic family of flies; the Fall Favorite; the Joe O'Donnell; the Night Owl; the Thor; and others which began life as local favorites are now tied and used on virtually all steelhead rivers. A few of the very good patterns for steelheads are enlarged versions of standard trout patterns, particularly such western patterns as the McGinty and Woolly Worm. Others came to steelhead country from overseas, or from eastern or Canadian trout and salmon waters; these include the Jock Scott, Silver Doctor, Highland Belle, and Montreal.

Winter steelhead fishing almost invariably requires special flies. Most of them are tied on hooks ranging in size from 1/0 down to #4, rarely as small as #6. In fishing for summer steelhead, you will be able to use trout flies in the bigger sizes, #10, #8, and #6. And in summer you will also be on the rivers when steelhead rise to the dry fly, so go prepared with a floating line and dry flies in big sizes. Summer steelhead fly fishermen can expect to be bothered frequently by trout and immature steelhead. These little fellows (half-pounders is the name given the steelhead) will seldom strike a lure and have trouble getting their mouths around a roe cluster bait, but they do hit single salmon eggs and they do love to snag flies in summer waters. Be kind to those that bother you; handle them gently and put them back into the water to grow up.

As a bonus, I'll pass on to you at this point a bit of dry fly arcana taught me by an angler encountered years ago on a tumbling western trout stream. I was having trouble keeping my dry flies on the surface, while his were making perfect, high floats. He noted my envious looks, and volunteered his secret. When you tie a dry fly on a #8 or bigger hook, work in a wisp of antelope hair in both tail and hackle. Your fly will not be ideally true to the book pattern, but the hollow-cored antelope hair will make it float high, without dressing, on even the roughest waters. So include antelope hair when you tie steelhead dry flies, and even the big sizes will stay afloat.

Floating is what you don't want your winter steelhead flies to do, of course. To make them sink better you tie them bulkier than you would build other flies, and to help them sink better as well as to hold a bucking steelhead, you put them on extra-heavy wire hooks forged by Allcock or Mustad in either the sneck or Model Perfect bend. Before the fast-sinking fly line appeared, weighted steelhead flies were very popular, since with the lines then available the only way really to get your fly down to the bottom was to wrap your hook with a course of fine brass or copper wire before beginning to tie on the body material. This took the flies down, but it also meant casting with tip-heavy terminal tackle, even when short leaders were used, and the weighted flies snagged bottom much more readily than do those tied conventionally. Today, not even the Pray Optics have extra weight in their big brass-ball heads.

You will be struck by a strong family resemblance between steelhead flies. Red, yellow, orange, and white predominate in their colors, and many have bodies of gold or silver tinsel. Streamers are heavily favored, with either bucktail or saddle hackle tips being used for winging rather than the more conventional quill sections. You'll also notice that steelhead flies tend to go to extremes; they're either very plain, or very fancy, with few of them in the middle area.

Some of them, such as the Red Rag, the Black Bug, and my own Cased Caddis, are so plain as to resemble the earliest fishing fly. This was described by Aelian, a Greek historian of the third century B.C., as being "a hook wrapped with wool, with two or three red feathers from a cock's wattle" tied around the red yarn. With it, Macedonians were taking what could only have been trout.

In the following list of winter steelhead flies, I've tried to include the best two dozen patterns that are to be relied on in any steelhead stream. You will find some variation in the dressings from one river to the next, but among these 24 you'll also be able to find something very close to many of the favored local patterns. All of them, in smaller sizes, are equally good in summer. All should be in your fly box, along with some scaled-up trout flies not on the list, but named later on.

BLACK BUG: Tail, wisps of black saddle hackle fibers; body, black chenille tied bulky; hackle, black saddle; hook, #2 or #4, 2x long. Sometimes an orange tail is used; the Bug becomes a Silver Hilton when wide-spaced silver ribbing is added. The pattern probably derives from the British Black Prince.

BUCKTAIL ROYAL COACHMAN: Tail, golden pheasant neck tip; body, peacock herl dressed over green wool for bulk; red silk band in center of body; wings, white bucktail; hackle, brown saddle; hook, #1, #2, #4, often 1x long. It is also tied on smaller hooks, but the big sizes seem more effective. Created from the English Coachman, a New York fly tyer named John Haley is credited with adding both the red band and the "royal" to the fly. The bucktail version is preferred in western streams to either the normal quill or the fan-winged fly. Variants include the Golden, with gold silk or tinsel band; the Silver, with silver pheasant neck-tip tail and silver tinsel band; and the Benn, with red saddle hackle fiber tail and a red streak in the wing. There is also a California Royal Coachman, tied with yellow chenille and silk body.

BUTCHER: Tail, scarlet bucktail; body, silver tinsel; hackle, black saddle; wings, black or blue-black; hook, #2, #4, or #6, 1x long. Also tied with black bucktail wing. Originally from England, the fly dates from about 1940, and was named for a Mr. Moon, famed as a fisherman, but a butcher by trade. Most silver-bodied steelhead flies probably derive from this old standard.

CASED CADDIS: Tail, wisp of medium-brown saddle hackle fiber; body, dark brown chenille tied full, tapering to a thick shoulder; hackle, medium-brown saddle, sparse, tied Palmer and clipped to about 1/8 to 1/4 inch; hook, #4 or #6. This is one of the few steelhead flies imitating a natural insect; it represents the grubs that cling to rocks on the beds of most steelhead streams.

FALL FANCY: Tail, none; body, wide silver tinsel; wing, white and orange bucktail mixed; hackle, orange, sometimes white or grizzly gray; hook, #2, #4, or #6 in 1x or 2x long.

FALL FAVORITE: Tail, none; body, wide silver tinsel; wing, orange bucktail; hackle, red saddle, sometimes white saddle; hook, #2 and #4, less often #6, 1x or 2x long. In the large sizes, the fly is often tied Optic-style with a brass bead head enameled black and having a red or orange eye-dot. Fluorescent bucktail is often used. I also like my own variant in which orange saddle hackle tips the length of the hook are substituted for the bucktail wings; this works well in smaller sizes, #6 or #8, 1x long.

GREEN BUG: Tail, none; body, one layer of green wool; rib, narrow gold tinsel; wings, eight to ten pieces of green wool as long as the hook tied streamer-fashion; hackle, grizzly gray saddle; hook, #2, #4 or #6, 1x or 2x long. The smaller sizes are very effective in low, clear water.

HIGHLAND BELLE: Tail, none; body, gold tinsel; rib, narrow silver tinsel; wing, orange saddle hackle tips over grizzly gray saddle hackle tips; cheeks, jungle cock eyes; hackle, white saddle; hook, #4 or #6, 1x or 2x long, less often in standard length. A traditional Scotch-British salmon fly that has proved its merit in taking steelhead; origin is unknown.

INDIAN FLY: Tail, yellow bucktail; body, mixed yellow and deep red wool tapered oval from tail to head; wings, squirrel tail a bit longer than the hook; hackle, ginger saddle. A very old steelhead fly, its originator was, by legend, an Indian guide from the state of Washington.

JOE O'DONNELL: Tail, scarlet saddle hackle fiber wisps; body, cream chenille tied bulky; wings, badger saddle hackle tips; cheeks, jungle cock eyes; hackle, yellow and scarlet mixed, tied full; hook, #2 and #4, 1x long. Variant is a Joe O'Donnell Gold, with gold tinsel body, usually tied on a #4 or #6 standard hook. Named for a famous pioneer steelhead fly fisherman, this fly was created as a joke by Bert "Butch" Wilson, during a relaxed after-fishing session at O'Donnell's fabled cabin near Orleans, on the upper Klamath. Tried by a few of the group the next day, the fly proved a fish-getter, and is now used widely. It has been effective on most of the steelhead rivers where it's been tried.

MC GINTY: Tail, wisps of mixed grizzly gray and scarlet saddle hackle; body, heavy black and yellow chenille in alternate strands, tied straight and rather thin; wings, white bucktail; hackle, brown saddle; hook, #2, #4, #6, all in 1x or 2x long. When tied on a standard hook, it usually follows the original version, thick body of yellow chenille with a broad black stripe at midsection. The bucktail wing on either long or standard hook is a western preference. The fly originated in the east, the streamer in Michigan.

MICKEY FINN: Tail, none; body, silver tinsel; wing, yellow bucktail with red bucktail streak through center; hackle, mixed red and yellow saddle, tied medium-long; hook, #2, #4, and #6 in 2x long. I also like a feather-winged variant tied with two white and one red saddle hackle tips substituted for the bucktail wing, tied on a #6, 2x long hook. Very good in slow-moving water.

MONTREAL SILVER: Tail, scarlet saddle hackle wisps; body, silver tinsel ribbed with claret tinsel or floss; wings, brown turkey or goose quill sections; hackle, claret saddle; hook, #4 or #6, often 1x long. This is a variant of the original Montreal or Canada fly, which is tied with a claret floss body and gold rib; the original is credited to Sheriff Peter Cowan of Quebec and dates from 1840 or 1850; the original resembles the Railbird, listed later.

NIGHT OWL: Tag, silver tinsel, tied long; butt, two turns of red chenille; body, silver tinsel; wings, white bucktail; hackle, orange bucktail; hook, #2; almost always finished Optic-style with a brass bead head enameled black and an orange eye-dot with a red center. The fly seems to have no appeal when tied on hooks smaller than #2, but in that size has proved almost irresistible to oversized steelhead.

OPTIC: This is a style of fly construction rather than a set pattern. The style was originated in the 1920s by Jim Pray of Eureka, California, the Optic feature being a large brass split bead clamped on at the head of the fly. Usually the bead is enameled black and has either a single eye-dot, white or orange, or a double dot, white/red or orange/red. Pray's first Optics were tied with deer-hair bucktail over gold or silver tinsel bodies, and the eyes were filled with solder to make the flies run deep. The deer-hair wing version first tied by Pray was soon followed by flies with white, orange, red, and mixed combinations of these popular steelhead fly colors. Optic flies are usually tied on #2 and #4, 1x and 2x long hooks, and modern Optics are not weighted with lead in their heads. Many standard patterns are tied with Optic heads for use in steelhead fishing.

PROFESSOR: Tag, gold; tail, wisp of scarlet saddle hackle; body, yellow floss; rib, narrow gold tinsel; wings, grizzly gray saddle hackle tips; hackle, brown; hook, #2, #4, #6. Variant, more popular than the original pattern for steelhead, is a wingless version tied with very full hackle of mixed grizzly gray and light brown.

RAILBIRD: Tail, yellow; body, light red or claret wool or floss; rib, claret hackle tied Palmer; wing, tip of squirrel tail or barred teal breast feather; hackle, yellow saddle; hook, #4, #6. Created by John Benn of San Francisco about 1890 for steelhead. It is an outstanding summer steelhead fly in its smaller size.

RED RAG: Lengths of red or scarlet wool tied loosely at the head; the sloppier this fly appears, the more effective it seems to be. Since its first appearance in the 1940s it has been joined by other "Rag" flies in other colors. All of them are tied on big hook, #1/0, #2, #4, in 1x and 2x long. The fly is favored by anglers using spinning tackle for fly fishing.

SHAD FLY: Tail, none; body, wide silver tinsel; wing, yellow bucktail; hackle, white; in front of the hackle a head is formed from two or three turns of red or fluorescent pink chenille; hook, #2. An excellent fly in the downstream areas and lagoons.

SHRIMP: Tail, the brown and white tip of a squirrel's tail fur; body, twisted red and orange chenille; rib, gold tinsel; wing, none; hackle, squirrel fur. The fly is tied like a humpbacked nymph, with the squirrel tail fur used as the tail brought up over the top of the body and tied in, then spread to form hackle. There are many variants of this extremely popular fly, but all retain the nymph form created by the fur being arched over the top of the body. Most common variants: all-red or all-orange body of chenille or wool; gold tinsel body tied over wool for bulk; silver tinsel body; red wool body with red saddle hackle tied Palmer closely spaced and clipped to about ¼ inch. Because of its bulky body and intricate construction, the fly is usually tied on #1, #2, and sometimes on bigger hooks, #1/0. The original Horner pattern for this fly used teal feather fibers for tail and back, but they could not stand up to the steelhead's strike. This is perhaps the best fly you can use in tidewater, and is not very effective more than a mile or so from the stream-mouths.

SURGEON or SURGEON-GENERAL: Tail, yellow bucktail; body, gold tinsel; wings, none; hackle, mixed yellow and orange saddle; ahead of the hackle a head or pair of eyes is made by tying on top of the hook two brass beads from a lamp pull-chain; hook, #2 or #4, 2x long. Variants include one with a silver body using nickeled pull-chain cord for eyes; with red tail and hackle in either gold- or silver-bodied versions. The fly was created by an unknown steelhead fisherman residing in San Francisco and made its first appearance in the middle 1950s.

THOR: Tail, orange hackle fiber wisps; body, bright red floss, wool or chenille; wing, white bucktail; hackle, medium-brown; hook, #2 or #4, 1x or 2x long. Jim Pray, who originated the fly, named it not for the Norse god, but for his fellow fisherman and neighbor, Walter Thoreson, who took an eighteen-pound steelhead on the fly during its first stream-testing. Starting as a local favorite, the fly has proved universally effective.

UMPQUA BELLE: Tail, red hackle fiber wisps; body, lower third yellow floss, upper two-thirds yellow chenille; rib, silver; wing, white bucktail topped with a streak of red; hackle, brown; hook, #2 or #4, 1x long. Another local that proved itself as a universally good pattern.

WONDER FLY: Tail, scarlet impala hair, very frizzy; body, light red or orange fluorescent chenille; wing, mixed scarlet and white bucktail; hackle, scarlet; hook, #2 or #4. Variants: wool body with gold or silver tinsel ribs; wing of the same fluorescent chenille used in the body; all-white or all-red wing.

Technically, each of the variants on the foregoing list could be classed as a separate fly, especially since so many differ to such a great extent from the ancestor pattern. But, the list is long enough as it is. Fly fishermen with bulging boxes remind me of the bearded fellow who was asked by a friend whether he slept with his beard under or outside the cover. On going to bed that night, the poor fellow tried the beard both ways, but couldn't remember on which side of the cover he usually left his whiskers while asleep. The problem returned each night to plague him, and he ultimately died of chronic insomnia. Anglers carrying too many patterns often spend more time changing flies than fishing, and their preoccupation over which pattern to present next causes them to miss a lot of sport.

Admittedly, the 24 flies on the list just given aren't enough to carry. My fly box is about as crowded with patterns in addition to the 24 favorites as is the box of the average fly fisherman, and it includes a lot of local favorites that I've picked up here and there and have been too lazy to weed out. But in addition to the 24 specialized steelhead flies listed, there are about a dozen more which I'd hate to be caught lacking. All these are standard trout fly patterns, some tied according to the book, others modified to streamer style for steelhead.

On the supplementary list, are the Green Drake in sizes #4 and #6; Improved Governor in #4; Jock Scott and Silver Doctor in #1/0, #2, and #4; Mosquito in #6 and #8; Parmacheene Belle tied streamer on #2 and #4, 1x long hooks; Woolly Worms in black-red, orange-black, and white-black on #1/0, #2, and #4, 1x long hooks; Dusty Miller and Gold Ribbed Hare's Ear in #4, #6, and #8; Gray Hackle in yellow wool, silver, and peacock herl bodies on #6 and #8 hooks; a couple of Badger Palmers with herl bodies on #4 and #6; and a few big, floppy spiders tied on #4 and #6 single salmon egg hooks. Patterns for all these can be found in any book on fly tying.

Strictly speaking, the twelve just listed aren't steelhead flies, but oversized trout flies. However, there are times when one or another of them will brighten a dull day by attracting a steelhead who doesn't know enough to strike one of the flies he's supposed to favor. They're worth carrying, if only as insurance.

For summer steelhead fishing, most of the steelhead patterns in sizes #6, #8, and even #10 hooks should serve you almost anywhere, but you might add to your box some of the supplementary patterns. And don't overlook trying your favorite trout flies, including dry flies, on summer steelhead trips. The McGinty, Parmacheene Belle, Professor, Railbird, Dusty Miller, Gold-Ribbed Hare's Ear, Thor, and the Gray Hackles, tied dry on #10 and #8 hooks, are especially good summer steelhead dry flies.

Even in early-season winter fishing, when the water in most rivers is low and clear, and the first winter fish are coming in to those streams not having their mouths closed by bars, small flies are often very productive. One memorable afternoon at Singley Pool on the Eel, when the water was like crystal and the winter fish just beginning to move upstream, I hooked seventeen on #10 and #12 silver-bodied gray hackle flies. These fish were wary, perhaps due to the low, clear water, and anything heavier than a two-pound test leader spooked them. Out of the seventeen hooked, I managed to hold on to nine, ranging from four to six pounds, and kept only one of the nine for the table since it was my first time out for the winter season.

Like all fly fishing, steelhead fly fishing calls for experimenting until you've hit on a pattern that appeals to the fish. Your ability to choose a suitable fly on the basis of insect life in or above the stream is lessened by the lack of insect life on most steelhead rivers; you have no real point from which to begin. Try the bigger, gaudier patterns first, and when you do change, make the change drastic, from silver to black or from red to white. Don't look to me for advice, because I'll be right alongside you going through the same fly-changing routine, trying to find something the fish like.

After you've found that appealing fly and had a fish or two touch it lightly, you can be pretty sure you're getting near the payoff. You make sure your footing is firm, because you've waded out near the head of the riffle as far as is safe; you're standing on gravel, and the heavy current not only shifts the gravel under your feet, but tugs at your knees, almost causing them to buckle. With that fresh fly solidly tied to your leader, you study the water, planning how to work it. You can start with a long cross-stream cast, lengthening each succeeding cast to let the fly drop a few feet downstream from the point where it hit water on the previous cast. This will allow the current to work the fly down and across the riffle in successively longer arcs; when you've reached the limit of your casting length, you can then begin with another cross-stream cast and shorten each succeeding cast, still working directly cross-stream, to let the drag of the current pull your fly across to the side on which you're standing in successively shorter arcs, until you're fishing only a few yards from your feet. If you've had no takers by then, you'll move downstream and repeat the casting pattern.

Now, you make that first long cross-stream cast, waiting nervously until you feel your fly bumping bottom as it begins to travel on its long arc down the current. You follow your line with the tip of your rod, holding the rod well up so that if and when a fish takes the springy rod will cushion the shock of the strike. When you finish your cast, you carefully spool all excess line onto your reel, so that line, rod, and reel are in a straight line and the fish, on striking, will take line right from the reel.

Downstream, your sunken fly is beginning to travel across the current; the movement of your line and the changed feel of the water's tugging tells you this. You're now in the strike zone, the area in which 85 to 90 percent of all hits on a fly occur. There's no guarantee that this zone will be productive; a steelhead may hit the moment your fly reaches bottom, or it may hit as the fly reaches the end of its cross-stream arc. You can be pretty sure, though, that a steelhead won't take a fly being retrieved against the current, so when the fly's at the end of its drift, close to the shore on the side of the riffle where you're standing, retrieve quickly, gathering your line into your left hand for the next cast. When you've reached the backtaper of your weight forward line, or your shooting head if you're using one, pick up the 30 to 40 feet of line that's still out with a series of roll-casts.

This is another standard casting technique; the pickup roll-cast begins with your rod held low and parallel to the water, is brought up with a quick smooth movement to the vertical, and the line thus retrieved rolled with a forward power cast along the surface of the stream. Two such roll-casts should bring to the surface the belly of your line, and it can then be picked up without straining your rod. A couple of quick false-casts while you turn your body in the direction your next cast will be made, and you're ready to shoot your line out once more.

Somewhere along that riffle you're so patiently exploring, a silver bullet with a crimson flush along its sides will smash into your fly. You won't see the strike you've been anticipating. Your first knowledge that you've connected with a steelhead will be the sudden tightening of your line at the same time that the fish breaks water in a splashing leap, downstream. Some fish don't leap, but bulldog during the entire fight. Most steelhead do a tail-dance, though, and that's when you'll want to drop your rod tip a bit to avoid a broken leader.

Whether it jumps or not, the fish will start downstream, and unless it's a small one, you're well-advised if you let it take line, keeping a minimum tension on your tackle until the steelhead stops. Then, you can persuade him to come your way, for that first tremendous burst of energy the steelhead's just expended has exhausted it momentarily. You'll gain a little line, and lose a little on the next run the fish makes. By this time, you should have waded out of the stream, and be on the bank, ready to run after your fish if you're forced to give up too much line during his next lunges.

From this point on, your job is to keep your line tight, but not so tight that a sudden movement by the steelhead will snap your leader. After a while, your rod-wrist will begin to ache, and at the beginning of one or another of its runs the fish will have set your reel spinning unexpectedly and the handle will have whacked your knuckles. And you'll have had another surprise, for the fish will have decided to try its luck upstream, and will head toward you faster than you can spool line on your reel.

But you persist, keeping on a gentle pressure, not enough to tear the gristle of the steelhead's jaw if it's lightly hooked, but just enough to keep that line tight and the fish's mouth open. Little by little the spool of your reel fills with line, and you realize the fight's going your way. You keep the pressure on, and soon there's only fifteen or twenty feet between you and the fish, and it's in the slacker currents close to the bank, where the fast water can't reinforce its strength.

You never really feel a steelhead give up. You'll lead the fish into the bank, to shallow water, waiting for it to make a final dash when it feels gravel scraping its belly. At this stage, you can afford to give line, for you have only a few yards out. Then, after that last desperate dash, you tighten line again, ready to take the few quick steps backward that will slide your steelhead across the shallows and up on the bank in one quick sweep. If you've taken a bragging-sized fish, or are hungry for fresh steelhead, slip your fingers into its gills, pick up a rock, and kill the fish cleanly with a blow to the base of its head. It's shameful to allow such a valiant fighter to gasp out its life painfully in an alien element.

If you're going to put the fish back to continue its spawning run, then wet your hands before you touch it; pick the steelhead up by the lower jaw, and remove the hook with a fast twist. Steelhead almost never swallow a hook; generally, they're jaw-hooked and hook removal is no problem. If you want to weigh the fish, a few seconds out of the water won't hurt it, but work fast. Then, step into the shallows and lower the fish into the water. Hold it under the belly with one hand, your hand still grasping its jaw, and turn its head upstream. Move the fish back and forth in the current, very slowly, until its mouth closes and its gills begin to function normally. Then you can release its jaw, still supporting it with a hand under its belly.

This is one of the greatest moments you'll ever experience in steelhead fishing. Holding the big silver form, a hand under the belly, the other hand over the back, you'll feel the fish's vigor return, feel the marvelous interplay of muscles that lie in layers under that shining skin. It is a feeling that brings you closer into kinship with a fish than any you've ever experienced. You will feel no regret, only a deep respect for a great fighter, when the steelhead, with a sudden twist, slips free of your hands and continues upstream to search for a mate.

8

Steelhead on Your Table

Whether you, as a successful fisherman, or your wife, now no longer a fishing widow, undertake the cooking of your catch, you will find steelhead on the table to be a delight. Their flesh is pink and moist, with a subtle flavor that is more delicate than salmon and richer than trout. Like any proper gentleman or lady welcomed to your table, the steelhead deserves your considerate attention; cooking it in an offhand or careless and thoughtless fashion is the equivalent of being discourteous to a guest.

Not that the steelhead is a difficult fish to cook; the reverse is in fact the case. It can be served perfectly plain, seasoned with nothing beyond a touch of salt and a sprinkling of lemon juice, or it can be poached in a finely seasoned liquid and richly sauced. Not only is steelhead delicious when cooked fresh, its flesh can be smoked, salted, or canned for later enjoyment. There are hundreds of ways to cook it, from simple to elaborate, and if you do not make the mistake of overcooking, which turns the flesh tough and dry, you will enjoy the steelhead you serve forth.

Before it can be cooked, the fish must be cleaned, but even this need not be done with undue haste. Most fish must be gutted immediately once they are out of the water; their digestive systems are so fantastically active that stomach acids will eat away their stomach's lining and taint their flesh if the fish are not cleaned at once. Like its *Salmo* cousin, the Atlantic salmon, the steelhead's digestive system comes to a virtual halt once it goes into fresh water; the fish eats sparingly, as we've seen, when it bothers to eat at all. In most of the steelhead you clean, the stomach will be empty and the intestines remarkably free of fecal matter, which simplifies your job of preparing the fish for cooking.

It's a constant source of surprise to me that so many experienced fishermen make a great or messy chore out of cleaning a fish. They go at the job reluctantly, almost angry at being forced to face such a task. Such an attitude brings to mind the old New England farmer whose son took a job as assistant in the village store during college vacation. After a few days, the youth began to complain that some of the work he was called on to do was menial labor, beneath the dignity of a college man. His father listened for a while to the son's complaints about having to sweep and dust, to stack canned goods and pile sacks of flour, then silenced them with a simple question: "Y'hired out for the money, didn't y'?" Any angler who catches and keeps fish should be prepared to clean them; if he objects to doing so, let him return the fish to the water while they still live.

One or two minutes is all the time required to clean any member of the salmonoid family, and even a big steelhead is no exception. Cleaning will take a few moments longer if it is to be done from the back, so that the steelhead can be plank-cooked or salted or smoke-cured, but at longest this is a five-minute job. There are no tricks involved, and you need only the scantiest understanding of the steelhead's anatomy. What's more, the quick-cleaning method can be used on any other game fish to make their preparation for the table fast and simple.

You must first learn one fact about fish physiology, and it applies to all fish in addition to steelhead. Once a fish is dead, do not let the fish touch water, or water touch the fish. All fish have a protective film covering their bodies; while alive, this covering makes them slick to handle, but not slippery. Dead, the covering dries rapidly, but if touched by water it turns to slime. Sand, twigs, or other harmless dirt should be wiped off a dead fish with a rag or paper towel. Do this, and you'll have no problem in holding on to the fish while you're cleaning it. If you slosh one in the stream or in a water-filled dishpan, or try to clean it while holding it under the faucet, you'll have a real wrestling match.

To clean a steelhead—or any other game fish and most rough-fish—run your finger lengthwise across its gills until you feel the bony head suddenly give to pressure. This will be a very narrow place between the fish's cheek and gills. Starting at the top of its head, run your knife down, following the soft line, to the point of the fish's chin. Now, find the bony ridge between gill-opening and the body; this is the operculum. Starting at the top of the body, cut the skin along this ridge to the belly. Do not cut deeply, all you want to do is slit the skin. Turn the fish over and make the same two cuts on the other side of its head.

Holding the head of the fish in one hand, with its bottom up, slip the tip of your knife into the point of its jaw. Run the knife back in a shallow straight cut to the vent. Spread the mouth of the fish wide open. At the top of the mouth, where the gills meet the head, there is a thin piece of gristle connecting gills and head. Cut this free. At the bottom of the mouth, below the tongue, there is an uncut piece of tissue holding the tongue to the jawbone; cut this.

Slip the thumb of the hand holding the fish into its mouth and get a firm grip on the roof of the mouth. Hook the first two fingers of your other hand into the cut you made in the belly and loop them around the tongue and comb-toothed rakers that form the opening to the fish's gullet. Pull these firmly and steadily back toward the tail. All the insides of the fish, the tongue, rakers, gills, gullet and intestines, will come out as a unit through the slit cut in the belly.

The end of the intestine will still be attached to the fish's anal vent, but when this vent is circled with the tip of your knife, it will also come away. If the fish is a female, be sure to separate the roe sac from the intestines before discarding them. If you don't want the roe for your own use in bait fishing, some fisherman friend will.

To complete the cleaning job, slit the heavy membrane at the top of the fish's cavity. It is filled with blood, usually in a single massive clot, which must be scraped out by running your thumbnail along the backbone through the slit you cut in the membrane. If the fish is a very big one, it might be necessary to use your knife or a spoon to scrape the blood out. Now, and not until now, wash the fish; while washing it, pull away the loose bits of the upper membrane that will still be clinging to the walls of the cavity. If the front fins didn't come away when you pulled out the gills and operculum, cut them off, and cut off the anal fins. Trim the dorsal fin off, level with the back, and chop off the finny section of the tail.

After you've practiced this technique of fish cleaning a few times, you should be able to prepare one for the table in less than a minute. It's a much less complicated procedure when performed than it appears while you're reading how to do it.

You can fillet your fish if you wish; the steelhead's size makes this operation very easy, and the meat lost when any fish is filleted will not matter as much as would be the case with a smaller fish. It isn't necessary to clean fish that are to be filleted. Lay the fish on its side on a firm, flat surface with its belly toward you and its head on your left. The knife you are using should have a fairly long, flexible blade, and be very, very sharp. Just behind the gills, make a cut at right angles to the fish's body, slicing down to the bone, and slanting your cut very slightly toward the tail. Turn your knife blade in the cut and with short sawing strokes begin cutting toward the tail, holding the fish's head in your left hand. Keep the blade of the knife at a slight forward angle, the tip pointed down toward your work surface. Cut as close to the ribs as possible; you should be able to feel your knife sliding over them.

When the flesh of one side has been removed, turn the fish over and reverse it, head-to-tail; the belly should still be toward you. When you cut the second fillet, with the same technique used in taking off the first, you'll find it necessary to cross your left hand over your knife-hand to hold the fish in place. This is clumsy, but much less so than trying to hold the body of the fish at an angle to the cutting board so that you can slant your knife to take off the thick chunk of flesh along the fish's back.

When your fillets are ready to be skinned, lay them flat on your cleaned cutting board, with the flesh side down and the tails on your right. Free a flap of skin at the tail end, and grasp it with your left hand while you ply the knife with short, scraping strokes to free skin from flesh. As soon as you've freed about an inch of the skin, start rolling it toward the head of the fillet, forming the roll with the fingers of your left hand and keeping it moving just ahead of the knife edge. Press down gently on the roll to keep the fillet from sliding along the cutting board.

Skin fillets only if they are to be cooked in a sauce; fillets to be plank-cooked, or cooked in a basket-grill over open coals, or broiled in the kitchen range, are easier to handle if the skin is left on. A steelhead has tiny scales and a clean skin that will not impart an unpleasant flavor during cooking, as will the skins of some coarser fish. After cooking, the skin will slide off easily, much more easily than when the fillet is raw.

Steelhead that are to be plank-cooked over a bed of coals from a driftwood fire along the riverbank, or that are intended to be smoked or salt-cured, should be cleaned from the back. A belly-cleaned fish cannot be spread flat because of the thickness of the flesh along its backbone. If plank-cooked, belly-cleaned fish will have a large under-done section; if smoked or salt-preserved, the curing is incomplete and the fish will decay from within.

To clean your fish from the back, use a freshly whetted knife to cut to the backbone on both sides of the dorsal fin. Carry both cuts to head and tail. There is a bony ridge of backbone running the entire length of the fish above the main backbone itself. Slip your fingers into these cuts just behind the fish's head and work the flesh down until the ribs are visible. Cut each rib with a heavy-bladed knife or with lineman's wire-cutting pliers. The fish is now opened to the tail section, and this must be cut free on both sides of the backbone.

Cut the body flesh free back of the gills, make a circling cut around the vent, and the head, skeleton, and intestines can be lifted off the flesh. There will be some membranous tissue still connecting flesh and bones, but this is easily pulled or cut away. The rib bones are then cut from the flesh with the tip of a knife.

Unless your home is in steelhead country and you plan to smoke or salt a number of fish each season, I suggest that you turn the cleaned fish over to one of the commercial smokehouses for processing. There are many small custom smokehouses and canneries close to the major rivers that specialize in this type of work. They will, or most of them will, accept your fish before cleaning, and do this job for you—for an additional fee, of course. While many steelheaders do smoke, can, or salt their own fish, they do it more as a labor of love than because they enjoy engaging in the tedious job of smoking. If you feel that you must try your hand at preserving the steelhead you've caught, there is ample literature on the subject to help you. However, after reading the books and pamphlets, find a fisherman who does his own steelhead smoking and talk to him about what you've read.

Quick-freezing is the best solution to preserving your fish for short periods of time, or for transportation home if you're on a distant river. Here again, I recommend that you take your cleaned fish to a commercial freezer plant, equipped to fast-freeze. Home freezers do not have the capacity to fast-freeze a fish as thick in the body as steelhead run, and unless the freezing is done quickly small ice crystals will form in the flesh of your fish and reduce it to a pulpy mass best consigned to the garbage pail. If you do freeze fish at home, freeze them in a block of ice by surrounding the fish with water in a long, shallow pan. A temporary container can be formed by bending heavy-duty aluminum foil to the desired dimensions. Be sure to do the freezing in two stages: first, freeze a half inch of water in the empty pan; then, lay the fish on this sheet of ice and pour icy water over it to cover completely, and freeze the fish into this icy jacket.

Quick-frozen fish wrapped in locker paper should not be thawed before cooking, but unwrapped and cooked with the time extended to allow for thawing. Fish frozen in an ice block should be freed from the ice under the water faucet and cooked at once. Before freezing any game fish, be sure to check locally on state laws that govern possession limits. In some cases, these limits apply to frozen as well as freshly caught steelhead. Since game laws can change rapidly and often, any summary of them written now might not apply by the time you're reading this, but it's a wise precaution to familiarize yourself with them at the place and time when they might apply to you. It's possible that if you don't you could find yourself in possession of an illegal number of fish.

By far the best way to enjoy steelhead on your table is to cook one in its natural, unpreserved state as soon as feasible after the fish has been taken from the river. There's a lot to be said for thin slices of smoked steelhead and for smoked steelhead paté served on thin slices of crisp toast for snacks or hors d'oeuvres; both are unique and delicious. But a fresh-caught steelhead cooked on grill or broiler and seasoned with the lightest possible touch brings to your mind the assertiveness of an ocean fish modified by the delicacy of a trout from fresh, cold water.

Steelhead belong to the family of fat fish, with much natural oil in their tissues. Because of this, and because of its size, the steelhead is not the best possible candidate for skillet cooking. Don't deny yourself the pleasure, if this is your favorite way of cooking fish. Just use discretion; an almost dry pan, and low heat, will deliver fillets or "steaks," thick slices cut across the midsection of the fish, the like of which you've never before encountered. Season the fillets or steaks only after cooking, with a tiny touch of salt and a sprinkling of lemon juice.

Deep-frying should be avoided when you cook steelhead. While the oils from the fish are light and delicate, they do not always combine happily with the fat in your frying kettle. Actually, your steelhead will be at its best on your table if it has been broiled, baked, or poached. In the first two methods of cooking, the fish should rest on a rack that will hold it above the bottom of the pan; the oil cooked out will collect in the bottom of the pan, and not be reabsorbed in the steelhead's flesh. When a steelhead is poached, its oil combines with the seasoned liquid used in this style of cooking and is modified in such a way as to enhance the fish's fine natural flavor.

Irv Urie of Medford, Oregon, a skilled and conscientious professional guide to the steelhead streams of the Pacific Northwest, has a way of cooking steelhead much admired by those who have gone on his drift trips. It can only be enjoyed at streamside, for it is based on the native alders that grow profusely along the banks of these rivers. A fire made from alderwood is allowed to burn down until its coals are suitable for cooking while the steelhead taken upriver are filleted and the fillets skinned. Dry dampened alder leaves and small twigs are then heaped on the coals, and in the dense smoke they produce the steelhead fillets, in basket grills, are smoked for several minutes. When the leaves and twigs are burned away, cooking is completed over the coals. Just before being removed they are brushed very lightly with butter.

By all means try Irv's method of cooking steelhead the next time you find yourself with a newly landed fish on the banks of a stream where alders grow. It will please you, but there are other ways of cooking steelhead which will please you equally as much. If you enjoy outdoor cooking, let me unblushingly recommend my own book on the subject, which includes not only recipes for steelhead and other fish, but for a complete array of other foods as well.* And certainly you don't need to cook steelhead outdoors to enjoy the fish thoroughly. Take it to the kitchen, if this is the place you prefer to do your culinary chores.

To broil a whole steelhead, place the cleaned fish on a rack in a shallow broiler pan. Leave the head on, or take it off, as you choose. If you cook it with the head on, you will be rewarded by two additional nuggets of flavor, the cheeks. These small morsels condense into one bite the quintessence of the fish's flavor, but many cooks prefer to remove the heads of the fish they cook, though it has no effect one way or other on the cooking. If your broiler pan is aluminum, fine; if not, line it with aluminum foil and it will not be

Cooking Over Coals, Winchester Press, $8.95

necessary to turn the fish during cooking—reflected heat will cook the side away from the heat source.

Preheat the broiler; if your range lacks a setting for this kind of cooking, turn it to the highest setting for ten minutes. Using an electric range, broiling is automatic; in a gas oven, regulate the flame to medium. Cook the fish seven minutes per pound if it is heavier than eight pounds; five minutes per pound is ample time for smaller fish. When done, the skin on the top side will begin to bubble up, and a fork or knife inserted along the dorsal line of the back and twisted will let no trickle of liquid out.

Take the fish from the oven and while it is still on the rack, slip off the skin from its upper side. The fins will come out readily; so will the spines of the dorsal fin if you choose to remove them. Have a heated platter at hand, and invert it on top of the fish; then, lift rack and platter together, and turn them over. The fish will be on the platter, skinless side down, intact and unbroken. It's a simple matter then to slip off the other half of its skin. Let each diner season his own portion, unless you want to sauce the fish while still whole; suitable sauces will be given later in this chapter.

Baking a steelhead should also be done with the fish resting on a rack in the pan. The main reason for baking a fish rather than broiling it is to serve it stuffed, with a combination of ingredients and seasonings that will add a new touch of flavor to its flesh. When planning the stuffing for a delicately flavored steelhead, you would naturally avoid using herbs and spices that would dominate the fish too strongly and destroy your ability to taste the flavor that nature has given it.

A lightly seasoned bread stuffing is ideal. Moisten the bread with a white wine, one of the good Rhines or a Sauterne or Chablis. Add a minimum of seasoning: salt, pepper, one of the lighter herbs such as rosemary or savory, or the famous go-with for fish, tarragon. Chop a shallot or two very fine, or use chives for a more pungent dressing, or the minced tops of a few tender young green onions. For both texture and flavor, put some diced fresh mushrooms or some slivered almonds into the bowl where the moistened bread crumbs and seasonings are being mixed, and break a fresh egg into the bowl to lighten and bind your stuffing. Mix all the ingredients together and put them into the fish's cavity, securing the belly-slit with a small skewer or a stitch or two of coarse thread. In a preheated 350-degree oven, bake twelve minutes for each inch of thickness you measure across the shoulder of your fish, just back of the head. Cook with your baking pan uncovered.

To poach your steelhead, you will need a pan long enough to take the whole fish and deep enough to allow its body to be covered completely with the liquid in which it will cook. There are special pans made for fish poaching, long and deep, with a rack on which the fish rests; the rack also allows you to lift it out of the pan carrying the cooked fish so that it will not be broken during transfer from pan to platter. These pans are nice, but you can do quite well without them, using an oval roasting pan or a long oblong baking dish. It may be necessary to remove the head to fit the fish into the pan, but this is a small matter. If you do not have a rack suitable for use with the pan you will use, fold cheesecloth double and let the steelhead rest on this while it cooks, then use the loose ends and sides of the cheesecloth to lift the fish out when cooked without its body breaking into small pieces.

Court bouillon is the traditional poaching liquid. It is prepared by mixing a bottle of your favorite white wine with two quarts of water, adding a large sweet onion, coarsely chopped, two sliced carrots, a few sprigs of parsley, two or three celery tops with the leaves left on, a bay leaf, and a sprig of thyme. Bring this to a boil in a deep saucepan, then reduce to a slow simmer and cook 30 to 40 minutes. Ten minutes before the liquid is to come off the heat, add two teaspoons of salt and a half dozen cracked peppercorns. When cooking is complete, strain the *court bouillon* into a bowl or into the pan in which you will poach the fish and let it cool. It will not be wasted after the fish is cooked, but used as a base for the sauce you'll serve with the steelhead.

When you're ready to cook your fish, and it is in the pan on a rack or resting on cheesecloth as already described, pour the cool *court bouillon* over it. The fish must be covered completely by the liquid; if it is not, add more wine and water to the pan. Bring the liquid to a boil, and when boiling begins, reduce the heat until it simmers very gently. Cook 30 to 45 minutes, depending on the steelhead's body. Test for doneness by lifting the skin at the belly-slit with a fork; if the flesh flakes readily, the fish is done. Lift it out of the liquid onto a platter or long shallow pan where it can drain while you prepare the sauce. It is a good idea to rest one end of the platter or pan on an inverted saucer or the handle of a knife so the liquid will collect in one corner or end.

There's nothing at all wrong, by the way, with serving your steelhead unsauced, just as it comes from the poaching pan. You'll find its flesh sweet and tasty, eaten with no accompaniment other than crisp French bread and butter, with a glass of the same type wine used in the *court bouillon*. Just remove the skin from the top, serve portions by separating the flesh with a dull knife and lifting them from the bones. When half the fish has been served, the backbone and ribs can be lifted free and the bottom half is ready for serving. Steelhead is good this way either hot or cold.

It's a matter of five to ten minutes to prepare a simple sauce to adorn and add piquancy to your poached steelhead. Put three cups of the *court bouillon* from the cooking pan into a small saucepan with one shallot that has been grated or minced very fine. Bring this to a brisk boil and cook until it is reduced in volume by one-half. Blend together a teaspoon of flour and a teaspoon of butter to form a smooth paste. Separate the yolks of two fresh eggs from the whites. Have ready a large pinch of nutmeg, a half teaspoon of salt, two tablespoons of rich cream or undiluted evaporated milk, and the strained juice of half a lemon—about one and a half tablespoons.

Strain your reduced *court bouillon* into a small saucepan and put it over very low heat. Flake the paste of butter and flour into the liquid in small pieces, stirring each time you add a bit until the piece is dissolved. Using a wire chef's whisk or a hand-sized electric mixer at the lowest speed, beat in the egg yolks, one at a time. Quickly add the seasonings and milk, stirring briskly, remove the pan from the heat, beat in the lemon juice and taste. Adjust seasoning as necessary. While the *court bouillon* is boiling, remove the skin from the poached steelhead and put it on a warmed platter. Pour the sauce over the fish, and serve.

By varying the sauce—or omitting it completely—you can make your steelhead dinner as elaborate or as simple as your tastes dictate. The simple white sauce just described can be made very fancy by the addition of chopped mushrooms, a sliver or two of truffle, a few shreds of pimento, used singly or together. It is equally tasty when served over a broiled steelhead, though you might prefer a more quickly prepared, simpler sauce such as Bercy Butter, which is also an excellent sauce to pass with baked stuffed steelhead.

Bercy Butter is prepared by chopping two shallots very fine and boiling them in a cup of dry white wine until the wine is reduced one-half in volume and the shallots are very soft. Remove from the stove and stir in three-quarters of a pound of butter, a tablespoon of finely minced fresh parsley, and a tablespoon of lemon juice. Season with salt and cayenne to taste; the sauce should be piquant, but not overpoweringly flavored with salt or pepper.

There are many other simple sauces based on adding herbs or seasonings to butter which go well with broiled or baked steelhead. *Maître d'hôtel* butter is made by adding chopped parsley, salt, lemon juice, and cayenne to melted butter. Anchovy butter is made by blending a well-drained anchovy fillet or two with butter. Mushrooms, shallots, herbs such as tarragon and chervil, seasonings such as mustard and prepared liquid sauces—all these and many more can be blended with softened or melted butter to make good, quickly prepared sauces for a broiled or baked fish.

Sooner or later, unless you have a large family, or have been foresighted enough to invite enough guests to dinner to demolish an entire steelhead at one sitting, you'll face the problem of leftovers. Fortunately, steelhead is as good cold as it is hot, whether the original method of cooking was sautéing, broiling, baking, or poaching. You will, of course, have protected the leftovers during their stay in your refrigerator by putting them in a covered dish, or by covering the plate with plastic film or foil.

Traditionally, the sauce that accompanies cold fish is Sauce Tar-

tare. This sauce goes equally well with hot fish, by the way, if you are firm about offering the original version, which has yet to be improved. The debased concoction served by most restaurants and the chemicalized kinds sold in jars are not only coarse in texture after being loaded with pickles, peppers, and miscellaneous garden truck, but so acid that they overwhelm your tastebuds and keep you from enjoying the flavor of the fish itself. Real Tartar Sauce is very simple and easy to prepare. Cream one hardcooked egg yolk in a tablespoon of fine light oil and beat this, together with a tablespoon of minced chives, into a half cup of mayonnaise.

Cold steelhead is also very compatible with other mayonnaise-based sauces. Sauce Chantilly is made by blending a half cup of mayonnaise with a quarter cup of whipped cream; Sauce Maltaise, by combining one and a half tablespoons of orange juice and a teaspoon of grated orange peel with a half cup of mayonnaise; Sauce Niçoise, by adding to a half cup of mayonnaise a teaspoon of tomato ketchup and half of a well-drained shredded canned pimento. If you enjoy garlic, serve Garlic Mayonnaise, made by boiling fresh garlic until it is soft, then creaming it into mayonnaise; here, your own taste must govern the proportions of your mixture.

Flaked cold steelhead can be beaten into eggs and scrambled; or used in a mousse or soufflé; or combined with breadcrumbs and a mere touch of grated onions, bound with a raw egg, formed into balls or croquettes or sticks and deep-fat fried. Large flakes of cold steelhead form the basis for a fine salad; toss them with finely diced celery, a scanty sprinkle of minced onion or chives, diced hardcooked egg, and shredded lettuce, all combined as tossed with a dressing made by thinning mayonnaise with a few drops of lemon juice or mild white wine vinegar.

In short, you can do anything with leftover steelhead that you would think of doing with canned tuna or salmon. The difference you will note with your first bite of the dish in which it's used will be that the steelhead tastes better. In part, this is the virtue of the fish itself, in part it is because its flavor has not been spoiled by undergoing the modification that occurs when any fish is subjected to the high heat and pressure needed in canning.

There are many other dishes which you, in your gastronomic ingenuity, are certain to discover or invent; dishes that will give steelhead the same stature on your table that it enjoys in the water. No matter how you choose to cook it, you'll find the steelhead's flavor to be distinctive and inimitable.

Whether your greatest angling enjoyment comes from the seeking, the catching, or from eating the fish you have caught, the steelhead can be depended on to provide pleasure.

9

Some Final Thoughts

As good as the hours on the stream are the evenings when companions who've shared the day's sport sit down to relax together and share experiences. There's usually a bottle of something and a pot of fresh coffee to be shared; during the evening a lot of lies are swapped, and even an occasional truth floats to the surface.

Unexpected new facets of character are revealed when conversation grows unguarded, and occasionally there's an argument, sometimes mild, sometimes bitter, but stopped short of lasting bad feeling. Always during the chatting, memories of former fishing trips are recalled, and of the companions who shared them. These last often bring an occasional moment of silence to the group, a tribute to friends who have joined the talk around the fire in the past, but whose voices will be heard no more. These aren't solemn evenings, though. There's more laughter than silence, and nobody takes a long face to bed when the coals have faded to black.

Somehow, in spite of the lies that bring the laughter, there's a basic honesty that prevails around the fireside after fishing. Since this is a chapter comparable to the fireside gathering, let me be honest about the subject of this book, and talk about the drawbacks of steelhead fishing. Not that what's gone before has been dishonest; dishonesty and inaccuracy are two of the things I've tried hardest to avoid. Any mistakes in the text are my own fault, the result of inability to interpret evidence properly and of jumping to conclusions not justified by facts, or of faulty judgment in deciding to omit some minor detail that should have been included and thus depriving you of a fact needed to help you form a judgment of your own.

But there are two kinds of honesty. There's the honesty of elision, that glides over a fact; and the honesty of full admission, that drags the fact out for examination. And a few facts still need to be dragged out.

First on the list is the unhappy fact that after you get steelhead fever, all other freshwater fish seem pale and uninteresting. You're not exactly blind to the virtues of trout or bass or walleye or muskie, but they somehow don't give you the kick they did before you met *Salmo irideus gairdneri*. You break out your light tackle in the springtime, and seek a river where the trout are active, or a lake where you know lunker bass are lurking, and you fish, but it's not the same. Even while you're playing that leaping rainbow or bulldogging bass, you find yourself thinking about how it's going to be six months later, when the steelhead start upriver.

Then we come to the second fact, which you can accept or reject as you choose. I've tried very hard to understate the case for the steelhead, not to build up the fish to such impossible dimensions that it couldn't live up to advance billing, and after a good performance have nothing left for an encore. I've tried not to exaggerate, but on rereading, some of the passages appear pretty lurid. They're not. Even employing calculated understatement, the steelhead's a hard fish to write about believably. The anglers who travel hundreds of miles every weekend to reach a steelhead stream for a day and a half of fishing will vouch for that.

And there's something else that might be considered a drawback, an attitude that is admittedly personal, but which I've found to be shared by many fellow anglers. When you get interested in steelhead, your interest spreads from the fish to its habitat. You become angry over the treatment of rivers, not necessarily steelhead streams, but all rivers. You come to look on the waterways as sources of life rather than as sluices for the disposal of human sewage and industrial debris. When you set out to do something about it, to change the concept that streams are an inexhaustible resource, self-perpetuating, which they unfortunately are not, you make people angry.

You step on political and commercial toes, and you find a few doormats that once bore the word "welcome" being rolled up when you approach. Ecology is, at this writing, a newly popular topic, and many who've come late to ecological propagandizing haven't learned, as those of us who've been through the mill have, that extremism isn't necessary. But those of us who've been trying to bring about greater ecological understanding and sympathy for conservation for periods of twenty years or more have learned some lessons. We've learned, for instance, that man is part of any ecology, and that man's needs can be made compatible with nature's laws and processes.

Many steelhead fishermen learned this through long years of work in trying to help revive a waning species. We learned that such efforts can be successful, and that much, if not most of the damage done to our rivers by past misuse and ignorance can be corrected—if enough people want it done. We've learned that only people working together can undo the damage caused by other people.

We've also learned that practical conservation and achieving a balanced ecology can be, in a lot of cases, a matter of people doing without. That's one of the lessons contained in an earlier chapter of this book, where the story of rebuilding steelhead runs in the state of Washington was told; how this was done by trout fishermen doing without their sport for a few months so that immature steelhead could reach the ocean without being taken prematurely by anglers.

Among other things, we've also learned that restoring ecological balance can't be done by passing laws at the Federal level, for the Federal government, through some of its bureaus and agencies, is one of the nation's greatest destroyers of ecological balances. We've seen little bureaucrats propagandizing for grandiose ideas in the name of "conservation" and "utilization" of resources such as rivers, and we've seen the destruction caused by some of those ideas when translated into reality. This destruction has stopped short of catastrophe, but in some areas the seeds for future catastrophes have been planted.

So, if any of the remarks made here or elsewhere in these pages encourage you to join in such efforts as those being made to preserve the integrity of a few wild rivers, put it down as a side effect of steelhead fishing. The steelhead isn't the only species that needs a few clean streams; people need them, too.

These, then, are the hazards of becoming a dedicated steelhead fisherman: the risk of having other fishing spoiled for you; the risk of getting a reputation for stretching truth past its breaking point; and the risk of being inspired to leap up on the ecological soapbox and thus be branded as the kind of kook who thinks fish deserve more consideration than people. And these are really the only drawbacks I've discovered in the pursuit of the steelhead. Oh, there's the weather, and the bruised knuckles, and the risk you take of getting overconfident on a wild river, but these are part of the sport, and not drawbacks in themselves.

So, I'll leave it to you. If you're a steelheader yourself, you'll understand what I'm getting at. If you're a stranger to the sport, but have tagged steelheading as something you'd like to try someday, don't say you weren't warned about the steelhead's knack of making addicts out of anglers.

Long before I began gathering material for the purpose of writing about the steelhead, I began asking questions just to satisfy my curiosity. Inevitably, this led me to authorities on the fish, and I'm very grateful to busy men like Clarence Pautzke and Loren Donaldson for taking time to reply to questions from a fisherman who, at that time, was just interested in finding out why steelhead behave the way they do. From fishermen encountered along the Pacific Northwest's rivers, and from others having expert knowledge of Great Lakes waters, I got a lot of answers, too. Not all of them were correct, but even an inaccurate bit of information often leads to the true answer to a query. Since I wasn't consciously doing research, I didn't keep a list of the names of these men, and the best I can do now is to thank them as a group.

For help given when my inquisitiveness passed from the area of personal curiosity to prewriting research, I owe a great deal to Dr. Ernest Salo, formerly head of the Natural Resources Division of Humboldt State College in California, and now at the University of Washington. Ernie spent a lot of time talking steelhead with me, was generous in loaning material from his files, and in reading and criticizing my first-draft manuscript.

Arthur S. Hale, biologist of the U. S. Fish & Wildlife Service; Captain Walter Grey and Jim LaFonts of the California Department of Fish & Game; and Arlo Dunbar of the Oregon State Game Commission's Alsea Fish Hatchery, also provided material and suggestions. Two other Oregon State Game Commission men, Dave Heckroth, Tillamook District Biologist; and Jerry A. Bauer of the Winchester station, were especially helpful in many ways. So, too, were their colleagues in the Great Lakes states. In Michigan, John Scott, head of the Fisheries Division of the Department of Natural Resources; Lud Frankenberger of the DNR Cadillac station; and DNR staffers Ron Rybicki, Ralph Hays, and Melvin Bowman aided materially and were generous with their time. Al Poff of Wisconsin's Department of Natural Resources and Don Woods and Joe Scidmore of the DNR in Minnesota provided valuable data on steelheading in those states.

Assistance in photographic matters was given by Pete Cornachia of the *Register-Guardian* in Eugene, Oregon; Ray Peart, of Eureka, California; and by Whitey Sawyer of the *Chronicle* in Muskegon, Michigan. For sharing the knowledge they use as professional guides and charter boat operators, I am indebted to Ralph Fairbanks of Wellston, Michigan, to Irv Urie of Medford and Dick Sturgill of Grants Pass, Oregon. Gene Hopkins, manager of the Medford Chamber of Commerce, and John McMahan, manager of the Grants Pass Chamber of Commerce, helped out with photos and advice.

For data on tackle, I'm indebted to Luther Hunt, Swede Malm, Harry Argovitz, and to Ron and Jim Spring, who loaned me rods, reels, and other gear from their stocks so that I could become familiar with the products of many more makers than would otherwise have been possible. There are some not mentioned in the text who provided answers on fishing methods and steelhead history; they include Jim Armstrong, Walter Thoreson, Wally Craycroft, John

Sten, Denny Wells, Buck Weaver, Jack Knowles, Dr. David Ellis, Lawrence Crosby, and John and Tom Seroczynski. Joe O'Donnell, who played host to a lot of fly fishermen at his fabulous cabin on the Klamath, and is perhaps the best fly fisherman for steelhead I've encountered, was responsible for much material. So were the fishermen who gathered at Joe's for sport and pancakes; Happy Hill, Larry Allen, the late Bob Titlow, and others.

Going back a few years, for fear I might not have another chance to do so, I must recall and recognize the kindness and patience of the late Hugh McClung and E. C. "Pop" Powell. These men, over years of happy association, shared with me their knowledge of the techniques of fishing as well as the mechanics of rods and lines and other tackle. More than any others, they got me started asking about the "whys" of fishing.

If it were possible to do so, and if she'd been less understanding, my wife would long ago have sued fish for alienation of affections, for during more than thirty years together there have been few times when I've not been carrying on a love affair with some kind of fish. Somehow, Aldine's always managed to overlook my preoccupation with trout, bass, steelhead, and others of the tribe; has endured my surly growls on fishless days and my overexuberance on good ones. She's accompanied me to wilderness camps, fishing resorts, and on long hikes to remote streams, and if the strain has been severe, she's been good sport enough not to show it. Since I often overlook expressing my thanks to her, I'd like to go on record now that I'm eternally grateful.

All those named and many more have contributed directly and indirectly to this book, with information, stories of their experiences, by example, or simply by providing the surroundings in which thoughts can be examined and perhaps grow into words in type.

Finally, in connection with the silvery fish that wears the crimson stripes of battle on its sides, I've tried not to rhapsodize too wildly about it, or to attribute to it virtues not earned. But I'm glad that the stage of concealment has passed, and it's out in the open at last, that I've been carrying on a love affair with *Salmo irideus gairdneri* since the day I first successfully wet my line in a steelhead river and saw a shining form break water in a white cloud of spray.

May all your love affairs be as pleasant.

Index